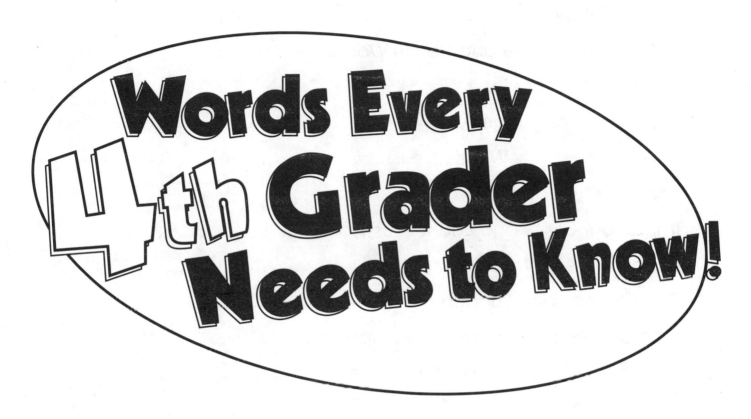

Words Every 4th Grader Needs to Know!

By Lee S. Justice

Frank Schaffer Publications
An imprint of Carson-Dellosa Publishing LLC
Greensboro, North Carolina

Table of Contents

Frank Schaffer Publications
An imprint of Carson-Dellosa Publishing LLC
PO Box 35665
Greensboro, NC 27425 USA

ISBN 978-0-76823-554-8
123107800

Dear Educator,

Welcome to *Words Every Fourth Grader Needs to Know!* This vocabulary series supports and supplements instruction in the content areas. The reproducible pages are designed to give students extra practice in using academic vocabulary. Academic vocabulary includes the subject-specific words that often challenge learners—words such as *legislative*, *friction*, and *hemisphere*—which they rarely encounter in everyday use. Terms like these may be challenging, but they are also essential to a student's ability to learn new subject concepts.

The 220 words in *Words Every Fourth Grader Needs to Know!* have been selected to match national education standards in the curriculum areas. The activities feature the vocabulary words in a variety of contexts so that students can activity think about how each word is used and make their own thoughtful connections about them.

Words Every Fourth Grader Needs to Know! is organized by content area. Start with any content area you wish. Then, provide students with the activity pages in order. An **Introduction Page** starts each section. It features a list of the words in that section, with two blanks before each word. Have students use the rating scale to evaluate their knowledge of each word before they do the activities and then again after completing the activities. **Explore a Word** activities have students focus on one word at a time to create their own associations. **Compare Words** activities show students how two related words are alike and different in meaning. **Make Connections** activities help students understand the relationships among words that are often used together. And **Play With Words** activities provide additional context and review in a playful format.

Additional features appear on some of the activity pages. **Word Alert!** activities point out word concepts, including structural elements, such as prefixes and suffixes, and word families with shared roots. **Look It Up!** activities help students develop dictionary skills as they investigate multiple meanings, word origins, and more. And **Challenge!** activities are starting points to get students thinking critically.

The **Student Dictionary** pages are organized by content area and support the activity pages in each section. Students should use the Student Dictionary as they work on each activity page. You may also use the Student Dictionary to model and review dictionary skills, such as alphabetical order, pronunciation, and parts of speech. Each section of the Student Dictionary ends with space for students to write more words and meanings from their subject learning. Reinforce and extend vocabulary knowledge by using the **Game Ideas and Suggestions** section, which includes ideas for the word cards provided at the back of this book, and game templates intended for small group or whole group activities.

We believe that with *Words Every Fourth Grader Needs to Know!*, your students will be well equipped with the necessary skills for success with subject-specific vocabulary.

Sincerely,
Frank Schaffer Publications

How to Use the Vocabulary Word Cards

Word cards with key vocabulary words are provided at the end of this book. These can be used as flash cards, also called *association cards*, to help students build quick associations between a word and its content-related meaning. Create additional word cards with all of the vocabulary words from this book or with additional words from your students' content-area learning. Incorporate the cards as you teach new vocabulary words. Use the cards to create a word wall. Or select one card and use that word for "Word of the Day" type activities. You can also use the cards for extension games and activities. Below are a few ideas to get you started.

 Know, Don't Know

Step 1: Student reads each word and definition in the pile.
Step 2: Student reads each word and tries to say its definition. If correct, the card goes in the "Know" pile. If incorrect, the card goes in the "Don't Know" pile.
Step 3: Student repeats Step 1, using only the "Don't Know" pile cards.
Step 4: Student repeats Step 2, and so on.
Step 5: After correctly defining each word in the original pile, the student tries again several days later.

 Quiz Show

Select a quizmaster to read each word or its definition to a panel of three contestants or to two teams of contestants. Each contestant or team has ten seconds to write the definition or the word. If they do so correctly, they earn a point. The winner has the most points at the end of a predetermined time period or number of words.

 Guessing Game

Display a selected group of cards, and play "I'm thinking of a word that. . . ." Offer students one clue at a time, including clues about word structure and relationships. Encourage students to raise their hands only when they are "absolutely sure" of the word.

Example of clues for the word *digestion*:
- I'm thinking of a word that has to do with eating.
- This word has a suffix.
- This word is often used with the words *stomach* and *esophagus*.
- This word names a process.
- What's the word?

Encourage students to try their hand at offering clues.

Important Math Words You Need to Know!

Use this list to keep track of how well you know the new words.

0 = Don't Know   1 = Know It Somewhat   2 = Know It Well

___ ___ centimeter

___ ___ circle graph

___ ___ circumference

___ ___ common denominator

___ ___ cubic unit

___ ___ cylinder

___ ___ diameter

___ ___ equation

___ ___ equivalent fractions

___ ___ factor

___ ___ horizontal axis

___ ___ inequality

___ ___ kilometer

___ ___ line graph

___ ___ operation

___ ___ percent

___ ___ plane

___ ___ prism

___ ___ probability

___ ___ pyramid

___ ___ radius

___ ___ rounding

___ ___ solid

___ ___ vertical axis

___ ___ volume

Explore a Word

Follow these steps.

1. Read the paragraph below. Think about the meaning of the **bold** word.

> Imagine tossing a penny into the air. The chance that it will land heads up is the same as the chance that it will land tails up. An even chance means that the **probability** is "one half" or "$\frac{1}{2}$."

2. What do you think the word means? Write your idea.

   probability: _____

   _____

3. Write a sentence with the word **probability**. Show what it means.

   _____

   _____

4. Check the meaning of **probability** in the Student Dictionary.

5. If your sentence in step 3 matches the meaning, put a ✓ after it. If your sentence does not match the meaning, write a better sentence.

   _____

   _____

6. Make a simple drawing to show the meaning of **probability**.

Compare Words

Look at the pictures and captions. Think about the meaning of each **bold** word. Then, check the Student Dictionary.

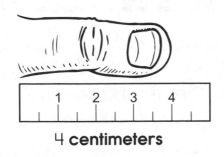

4 **centimeters**

4 **kilometers**

Fill in the chart with your own ideas.

Length or Distance	Example
1 centimeter (cm)	thickness of a picture book
5 kilometers (km)	
10 cm	
10 km	
	distance between school and home
	length of a pencil

🔍 Word Alert!

A prefix is a word part added before a word. Measurement words often have prefixes.

Prefix	Word	Meaning
centi- means "one hundredth"	*meter*	*centimeter* means "one-hundredth (.01) of a meter"
kilo- means "one thousand"	*meter*	*kilometer* means "one thousand (1,000) meters"

A liter bottle holds about 4 cups of water.

1. How much is in a centiliter? _____

2. How much is in a kiloliter? _____

Compare Words

Read the sentences below. Think about the meaning of each **bold** word. Then, check the Student Dictionary.

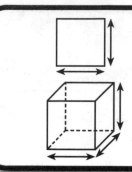

A **plane** figure is flat and has only length and width. A square is a plane figure.

A **solid** figure has length and width. It also has depth, or thickness. A cube is a solid figure.

Label each figure with the word *plane* or *solid*.

1.
   plane

2.
   plane

3.
   solid

4.
   solid

5.
   plane

6.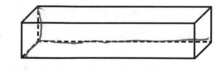
   solid

 Look It Up!

Each meaning of a word is numbered in a dictionary entry. Look up the word *plane* in a classroom dictionary. Write the meaning that fits with this page.

Completly level or flat.

Words Every Fourth Grader Needs to Know!

Compare Words

Look at the examples and captions. Think about the meaning of each **bold** word. Then, check the Student Dictionary.

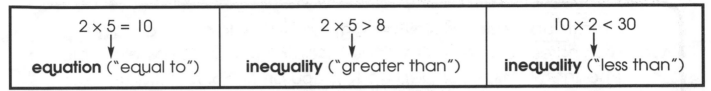

$2 \times 5 = 10$	$2 \times 5 > 8$	$10 \times 2 < 30$
equation ("equal to")	**inequality** ("greater than")	**inequality** ("less than")

How are equations and inequalities alike? How are they different? Fill out the chart. Include at least two ways they are alike. List as many differences as possible.

Equation	Both	Inequality

🔍 Word Alert!

The words *equation* and *inequality* share the letters *equ*. This group of letters comes from a Latin root that means "even" or "level."

Many other words, such as *equal* and *equator*, share this Latin root. With a partner, take turns explaining what each word means. What is alike about all the meanings?

_____

_____

Make Connections

Read the paragraph below. Think about the meaning of each **bold** word. Then, check the Student Dictionary.

> A math **operation** is any action, such as adding or dividing, which involves numbers. One operation is **rounding**. For example, the amount $4.59 is rounded up to $4.60 or to $5.00. $4.32 is rounded down to $4.30 or to $4.00.

Pretend that you are a teacher! Complete the dialogue with the correct answers.

Student: I know that adding, dividing, and rounding are math operations. What are some other math operations?

Teacher: _____

Student: When should I use rounding?

Teacher: _____

_____

Student: How do I round 627 to the nearest ten?

Teacher: _____

_____

Student: How do I round 627 to the nearest hundred?

Teacher: _____

_____

Take turns reading the dialogue with a partner. Are there any changes you should make to it? If so, show those changes.

Make Connections

Look at the pictures and captions. Think about the meaning of each **bold** word. Then, check the Student Dictionary.

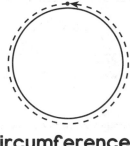
circumference

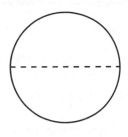
diameter

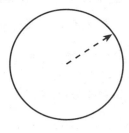
radius

Circle *Yes* or *No* for each question. Write your reason on the line.

1. Is the diameter of a circle half the length of the radius?   Yes   No

   _____

2. Does a radius touch the center of a circle?   Yes   No

   _____

3. Is the circumference a straight line?   Yes   No

   _____

4. Does this picture show diameter?   Yes   No

   _____

5. Does this picture show a radius?   Yes   No

   _____

6. Could a square have a circumference?   Yes   No

   _____

Make Connections

Read the sentences below. Think about the meaning of each **bold** term. Then, check the Student Dictionary.

> The fractions $\frac{3}{4}$, $\frac{9}{12}$, and $\frac{75}{100}$ are **equivalent fractions**.
>
> The fractions $\frac{1}{4}$ and $\frac{3}{4}$ have a **common denominator** of 4.
>
> A **percent** has 100 in the denominator. $\frac{5}{100} = .05 = 5\%$; $\frac{75}{100} = .75 = 75\%$.
>
> In the number sentence $3 \times 5 = 15$, the numbers 3 and 5 are **factors** of 15.

Follow the directions to draw or write.

1. Draw a picture to show a cookie cut in half. Label one piece $\frac{1}{2}$. Label the other piece with an equivalent fraction.

2. Draw a square. Shade 25 percent of it. Draw stripes in 75 percent of it.

3. Fractions can be added only if they have a common denominator. Write a number sentence to show what that means.

_____

4. The number 1 is a factor of every whole number. Write two number sentences to show what that means.

_____

 Challenge!

Use factors to change two equivalent fractions into two fractions with a common denominator. Show your work.

Words Every Fourth Grader Needs to Know!

Make Connections

Read the paragraph below and look at the pictures. Think about the meaning of each **bold** term. Then, check the Student Dictionary.

> A cube is an example of a solid figure. A **pyramid**, **prism**, and **cylinder** are other solid figures. The space inside of a solid figure is called the **volume**. Volume is measured in **cubic units**, such as cubic inches, cubic feet, and cubic meters.

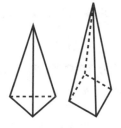
pyramids

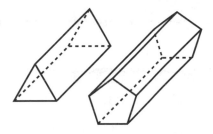
prisms

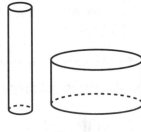
cylinders

Complete each sentence with one word.

1. Each face of a pyramid is the shape of a _____.

2. Each face of a prism has _____ sides.

3. Each base of a cylinder is the shape of a _____.

4. Multiply the length by the width by the depth to find the _____ of a box.

5. One common object with a volume of about 8 cubic feet is a _____.

Draw a cube. Label its length, width, and depth. Write a sentence about it using the words *cubic units* and *volume*.

_____

_____

_____

_____

Make Connections

Name _____

Read the sentences below. Think about the meaning of each **bold** term. Then, check the Student Dictionary.

> A **circle graph** is sometimes called a *pie chart*. It is broken into sections that show the parts of a whole, just like the slices of a pie.
>
> A **line graph** shows changes over time. The labels on the **horizontal axis** show units of time, such as days or months. The labels on the **vertical axis** show how much or how many.

Look at the circle graph. Label the sections with your own ideas. Then, write a sentence to explain what the graph shows. Use the term *circle graph* in your sentence.

Favorite Outdoor Activities of 150 Students

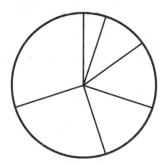

_____

_____

_____

_____

_____

Look at the line graph. Label the horizontal axis and the vertical axis with your own ideas. Draw a line on the graph. Then, write a sentence to explain what the graph shows. Use the term *line graph* in your sentence.

How Much Did I Read This Week?

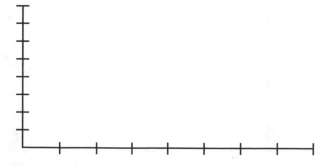

_____

_____

_____

_____

14

Words Every Fourth Grader Needs to Know!

Make Connections

Read each pair of vocabulary words. Write the words where they fit in the sentences. Check the Student Dictionary for any meanings that you need.

1. probability   percent

   There is a thirty _percent_ chance of rain today. That means, the _probability_ that it will rain is about $\frac{1}{3}$.

2. cylinder   volume

   A soup can is in the shape of a _cylinder_. The _volume_ tells how much soup the can holds.

3. equation   operation

   You solve an _equation_ by performing each step of an _operation_.

4. circle graph   inequality

   One section of the _inequality_ is greater than all the others. This _circle graph_ can be shown with the symbol >.

5. centimeter   plane

   The artist measured each side of the _plane_ figure. One side was a _centimeter_ shorter than the other sides.

6. rounding   diameter

   The _diameter_ of our round swimming pool is exactly 2.36 meters. We can use _rounding_ to say that it is about 2.4 meters across.

Choose two of the vocabulary words on this page. Write them in a sentence. Then, write the sentence again on another sheet of paper. Leave blank lines for the two words. Challenge a partner to complete your sentence.

_____

_____

Play With Words

Code Words

Choose the word that fits in each sentence. Circle its letter.

1. A wheel has a _e_.
   - **d** prism
   - **(e)** circumference
   - **f** vertical axis

2. Find the sum of this _s_.
   - **q** percent
   - **r** rounding
   - **(s)** equation

3. Three is a _t_ of six.
   - **(t)** factor
   - **u** kilometer
   - **v** circumference

4. One-hundredth is a small _j_.
   - **i** probability
   - **(j)** factor.
   - **k** diameter

5. A sphere is a _m_ figure.
   - **l** plane
   - **(m)** solid
   - **n** radius

6. Measure your height in _a_.
   - **(a)** centimeters
   - **b** kilometers
   - **c** diameters

7. One-half is equal to fifty _t_.
   - **s** equivalent fractions
   - **(t)** percent
   - **u** cubic units

8. The _e_ shows a steep drop in temperature.
   - **(e)** line graph
   - **f** circle graph
   - **g** probability

Write the circled letters in order. You will find a word that tells what people often do to figure out how much or how many.

Name _____

Play With Words

Letter by Letter

Choose the word that fits with each clue. Write it letter by letter. Some letters will be inside circles.

radius	prism	cubic	inequality
pyramid	rounding	cylinder	kilometer

1. 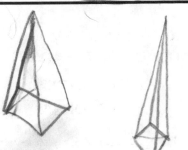   p (y) r a m i d

2. 4 3 6 → 440   r (o) u n d i n g

3. A balloon holds _____ centimeters of air.   c (u) b i c

4. 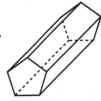   r a (d) i u s

5. a 10-_____ race   k (i) l e m e t e r

6.   c y l i n (d) e r

7.    p r (i) s m

8. 3 × 4 > 5 × 2 = 120   i n e q u a l i (t) y

Write the circled letters in order on the blanks to find a message.

you did it!

Play With Words

Compound Word Mix-Up

Unscramble the letters to write a math term that matches each picture or example. The term will be a compound word.

1.
   icceri *(circle)* pargh

   circle   graph

2. $\frac{1}{4}$, $\frac{2}{8}$, $\frac{25}{100}$ quanveilet   noictrafs

   equivalent fractions

3. $\frac{1}{7}$, $\frac{3}{7}$, $\frac{5}{7}$ moncom   ratnonimoed

   common denominator

4. 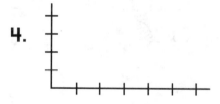   inel   garph

   line   graph

5. *5. 3 148 367*   zorhifloan   sixa

   horizontal axis

6.   trelicav   ixas

   vertical axis

Caption Match

Draw a circle with a radius of about 2 centimeters. Use this equation and rounding to help you measure: 1 inch = 2.54 centimeters. Shade about 20 percent of your plane figure to make it look like a solid figure. Then, add any details you like.

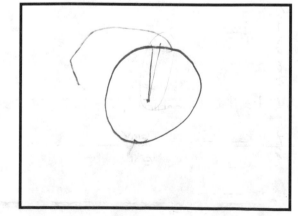

Important Science and Health Words You Need to Know!

Use this list to keep track of how well you know the new words.

0 = Don't Know   1 = Know It Somewhat   2 = Know It Well

___ 2 artery
___ 2 cell
___ 2 circuit
___ 2 conductor
___ 2 crust
___ 2 digestion
___ 2 electric current
___ 2 erupt
___ 2 erosion
___ 2 esophagus
___ 2 fault
___ 2 fossil
___ 2 frequency
___ 0 igneous
___ 1 insulator
___ 2 intensity
___ 2 large intestine
___ 2 lava

2 ___ magma
2 ___ mantle
2 ___ metamorphic
2 ___ nucleus
2 ___ organ
2 ___ pitch
2 ___ rock cycle
1 ___ sedimentary
2 ___ small intestine
2 ___ stomach
2 ___ tissue
2 ___ vein
2 ___ vibrate
2 ___ volcano
2 ___ volume
2 2 wavelength
2 2 weathering

Explore a Word

Follow these steps.

1. Read the paragraph below. Think about the meaning of the **bold** word.

> Long ago, animals walked across a muddy shore. The mud hardened, and the animals' tracks remained. Today, scientists study these tracks and other **fossils** to learn about prehistoric life.

2. What do you think the word means? Write your idea.

fossil: _I think fossil means somthing that is from a long But it is still here today._

3. Write a sentence with the word **fossil**. Show what it means.

I saw a Leaf fossil and it was was a little green and red.

4. Check the meaning of **fossil** in the Student Dictionary.

5. If your sentence in step 3 matches the meaning, put a ✓ after it. If your sentence does not match the meaning, write a better sentence.

I was at the Beach and i found the fossil of a horseshoe crab in a rock.

6. Make a simple drawing to show the meaning of **fossil**.

Words Every Fourth Grader Needs to Know!

Compare Words

Read the paragraph below. Think about the meaning of each **bold** word. Then, check the Student Dictionary.

> Heat, cold, rain, wind, and living things all act on rocks and soil. Heat and cold can crack a rock in half. Plant roots can cause a rock to break into smaller pieces. These kinds of changes are called **weathering**. Water can also carry rocks and soil from one place to another. Wind can blow soil to new places, too. The movement of rocks and soil is called **erosion**.

Read each sentence. Is it an example of erosion or weathering? Circle the correct answer.

1. A river carries soil all the way to the ocean.
   erosion   weathering

2. A tree grows from a small crack in a rock, making the crack wider.
   erosion   weathering

3. Rain washes soil and small rocks down a mountainside.
   erosion   weathering

4. Hot summers and icy winters cause a boulder to split apart.
   erosion   weathering

5. Farmers worry about a flood that is washing good soil away.
   erosion   weathering

Look at this picture of a mountain. Add arrows and captions to tell about weathering and erosion.

erosion   weathering

Compare Words

Read the paragraph below. Think about the meaning of each **bold** word. Then, check the Student Dictionary.

> At this very moment, blood rich in oxygen is being pumped from your heart to every part of your body. It travels through tubes that start out wide and branch into tiny ones. Each tube is called an **artery**. After the blood delivers its oxygen, it returns to the heart. The tubes that carry blood back to the heart are called **veins**.

Circle the word that completes each sentence.

1. Bright red blood carries oxygen through (arteries/veins) from the heart.

2. Brownish blood does not have much oxygen. It travels back to the heart through (arteries/veins).

3. The walls of (arteries/veins) squeeze and swell to help the heart send blood through the body.

4. Small (arteries/veins) join together to form bigger ones. One large tube from the upper part of the body and another large tube from the lower part of the body empty into the heart.

5. The heart pumps blood directly into the aorta. The aorta is the biggest (artery/vein) in the body.

Draw a simple diagram to show how blood flows from and to the heart. Include the vocabulary words in your captions.

Words Every Fourth Grader Needs to Know!

Make Connections

Read the paragraph below. Think about the meaning of each **bold** term. Then, check the Student Dictionary.

> Flip the switch, and an **electric current** is on the move! It flows through a wire to the light bulb and then back again. The path is called a **circuit**. A metal wire is a good **conductor** of electricity. Plastic around the wire is a good **insulator**.

The bulb in this picture won't light! Write instructions on how to turn it on. Use all of the vocabulary words in your instructions.

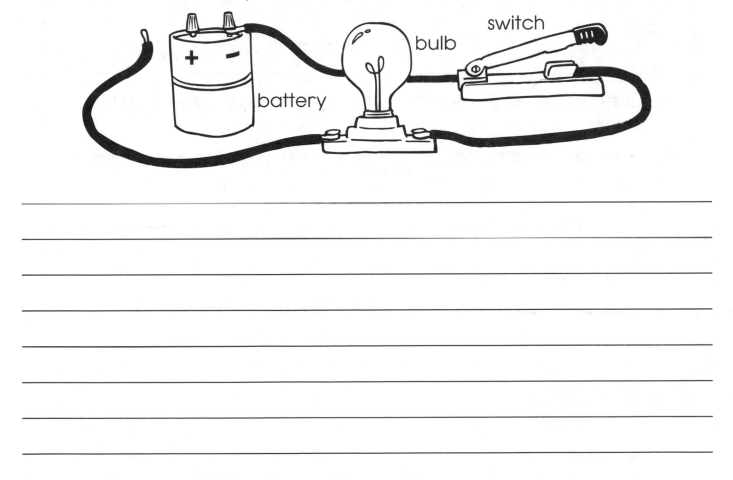

switch

bulb

battery

_____

_____

_____

_____

_____

_____

_____

 Look It Up!

The word *conductor* has more than one meaning. Use a classroom dictionary to find three meanings of the word. On another sheet of paper, draw three pictures to show the different meanings.

Make Connections

Read the paragraphs below. Think about the meaning of each **bold** word. Then, check the Student Dictionary.

> Imagine drilling a hole to the center of the Earth. What would you find? First, you would drill through the **crust**. This outer layer may be up to 40 kilometers (25 miles) thick. The crust and the uppermost part of the **mantle** beneath it are broken into giant plates. The edges of some plates may slide against each other to form a **fault**, or break. Earthquakes happen along faults.
>
> Earth's plates move because they lie on super-hot rocks that flow like thick liquid. This molten rock makes up the rest of the mantle, which is about 2,900 kilometers (1,800 miles) thick.
>
> Keep drilling. First, you'll pass through the Earth's thick outer core and then through its inner core. Finally, you'll have reached the center. That is, if your drill is 6,400 kilometers (almost 4,000 miles) long!

Draw a diagram to show the Earth's different layers. Include the vocabulary words in your captions.

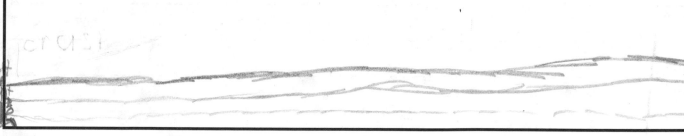

 Look It Up!

Science words often have special meanings, different from the everyday meanings of the same words. Look up the vocabulary words in a classroom dictionary. Write the number and meaning that fit with science.

1. crust _____

2. fault _____

3. mantle _____

Words Every Fourth Grader Needs to Know!

Make Connections

Read the sentences below. Think about the meaning of each **bold** word. Then, check the Student Dictionary.

> Molten rock from below the Earth's crust is called **magma**. When magma **erupts** from a **volcano**, it shoots out as red-hot **lava**, cinders, and ash.

Use the vocabulary words in captions to label this diagram.

🔍 Word Alert!

The root *rupt* comes from a Latin word meaning "to break." Use the word *break* to describe each word below.

1. erupt _____

2. disrupt _____

3. interrupt _____

4. rupture _____

Make Connections

Look at the diagram. Think about the meaning of each **bold** term. Then, check the Student Dictionary.

This diagram shows the **rock cycle**.

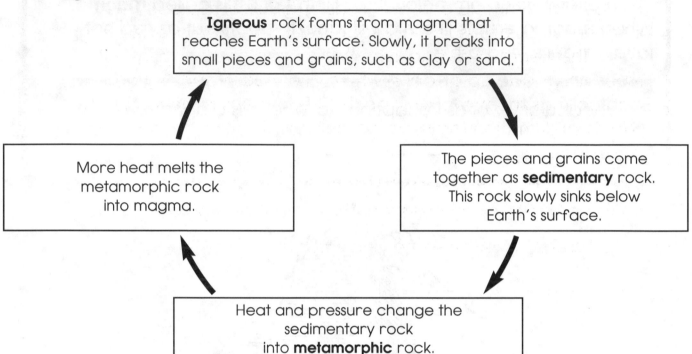

Igneous rock forms from magma that reaches Earth's surface. Slowly, it breaks into small pieces and grains, such as clay or sand.

More heat melts the metamorphic rock into magma.

The pieces and grains come together as **sedimentary** rock. This rock slowly sinks below Earth's surface.

Heat and pressure change the sedimentary rock into **metamorphic** rock.

Underline the better ending to each sentence.

1. You would expect to find igneous rock
   A. on the slopes of a volcano.
   B. on land that was once a lake bottom.

2. An example of sedimentary rock is
   A. sandstone, formed from layers of sand.
   B. granite, formed from magma beneath the Earth's surface.

3. An example of metamorphic rock is
   A. shale, formed from layers of clay.
   B. slate, formed from buried shale.

4. A complete rock cycle probably takes
   A. millions of years.
   B. hundreds of years.

Make Connections

Read the paragraph below. Think about the meaning of each **bold** word. Then, check the Student Dictionary.

Bone and muscle are two kinds of **tissue** in the body. Different kinds of tissue work together to help an **organ** perform its job. The heart, eye, and liver are examples of organs. All tissues are made up of **cells**, which are much too tiny to see. Each cell has many working parts. The **nucleus** is the largest part. It holds information that tells the cell how to grow, work, and reproduce.

Circle *Yes* or *No* for each question. Write your reason on the line.

1. Do all tissues have the same kinds of cells?   Yes   No

_____

2. Is the stomach an organ?   Yes   No

_____

3. Do organs form tissues?   Yes   No

_____

4. Is a nucleus smaller than a cell?   Yes   No

_____

Label each picture with a vocabulary word.

1. 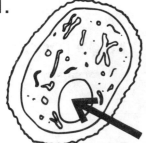   2.    3.    4.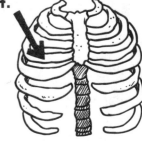

_____   _____   _____   _____

Make Connections

Look at the diagram. Think about the meaning of each **bold** word in the captions. Then, check the Student Dictionary.

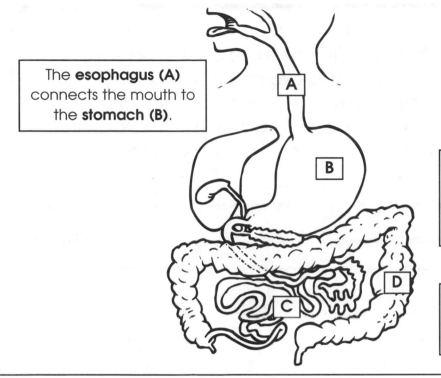

The **esophagus (A)** connects the mouth to the **stomach (B)**.

Unfolded, the **small intestine (C)** would stretch across a room. Nutrients pass through it into the bloodstream.

The **large intestine (D)** prepares waste to leave the body.

Food changes into nutrients that fuel the body's cells. This process is called **digestion**.

Use the vocabulary words to complete the paragraphs. Use some words more than once.

The (1.) _____ of food begins in the mouth. As you chew, saliva moistens the food and prepares it for swallowing. With a gulp, you send the food down your (2.) _____.

Muscles in your (3.) _____ push the food downward, until it enters the (4.) _____. Here, muscles churn the food into liquid. Acids and other chemicals act on the food, too. Chemical actions continue in the next organ, called the (5.) _____.

The (6.) _____ is where most nutrients enter the blood and travel to the rest of your body. Material that cannot be used as fuel passes into the (7.) _____ and leaves your body as waste. The whole process of (8.) _____ takes about 24 hours.

Make Connections

Read the paragraphs below. Think about the meaning of each **bold** word. Then, check the Student Dictionary.

> When something **vibrates**, it produces sound energy. The energy moves along in waves. The **intensity** of the waves is a measure of their power. The higher the intensity, the greater the **volume**, or loudness, of the sound.
>
> Sound also has **pitch**, or highness or lowness. The distance between any two waves is called the **wavelength**. Wavelengths are shorter in something that vibrates very quickly, or at a high **frequency**. The higher the frequency, the higher the pitch.

Complete each sentence with information about sound. Include the vocabulary word in your answer.

1. intensity
   I hit the drum as hard as I could, but _____

   _____.

2. frequency
   When I want to play a high note, I _____

   _____.

3. vibrate
   When I tap a glass with a spoon, _____

   _____.

4. volume
   I blew gently into the horn because I _____

   _____.

5. pitch
   Our music teacher sings in a voice that has _____

   _____.

6. wavelength
   Some animals can hear sounds that we can't, because they _____

   _____.

Make Connections

Read each pair of vocabulary words. Write the words where they fit in the sentences. Check the Student Dictionary for any meanings that you need.

1. sedimentary rocks   fossils

   Some _____ were once mud at the bottom of ancient seas. They often contain _____ of shellfish.

2. weathering   erosion

   Wind, snow, and other kinds of _____ can change the size and shape of a rock. Pieces of the rock may wash away through _____.

3. digestion   organ

   The stomach is just one _____ that is needed for the _____ of food.

4. veins   arteries

   _____ carry blood to all parts of the body.
   _____ carry blood back to the heart.

5. conductor   insulator

   Aluminum foil is a good _____ of electricity, and plastic wrap is a good _____.

6. vibrate   pitch

   Pluck a short string, and it will _____ faster than a longer string. The short string has a higher _____.

Choose two of the vocabulary words on this page. Write a sentence with them.

_____

_____

Make Connections

Read each list of vocabulary words. Cross out the word that does not fit with the others. Explain why this word does not belong. Check the Student Dictionary for any meanings that you need.

1. magma, lava, igneous, nucleus

   _____

2. circuit, rock cycle, volcano, mantle

   _____

3. small intestine, artery, crust, esophagus

   _____

4. metamorphic, erupt, igneous, sedimentary

   _____

5. volume, intensity, fault, pitch

   _____

6. cell, tissue, organ, mantle

   _____

 Challenge!

Write a silly riddle using a vocabulary word that has more than one meaning. For example, *What did the scientist say after failing to predict an earthquake? (Don't blame me, it's not my fault!)*

_____

_____

_____

_____

Play With Words

Code Words

Choose the word that fits in each sentence. Circle its letter.

1. Miners dig deep into the Earth's ___.
   t nucleus
   u magma
   v crust

2. The ___ of sound is its loudness.
   n frequency
   o intensity
   p conductor

3. Dinosaur bones are examples of ___.
   j erosion
   k organs
   l fossils

4. Lava spilled out of the ___ volcano.
   c erupting
   d mantle
   e metamorphic

5. Hit a drum to make it ___.
   a vibrate
   b volume
   c pitch

6. Electric current does not flow through ___.
   m a circuit
   n a conductor
   o an insulator

7. Living tissue is made of ___.
   h veins
   i cells
   j esophagus

8. Close the ___ to turn on the light.
   a mantle
   b nucleus
   c circuit

Write the circled letters in order. You will find a word that describes rocks, a mountain, an island, or a fiery temper!

_____

Play With Words

Letter by Letter

Choose the word that fits with each clue. Write it letter by letter. Some letters will be inside circles.

intestine	nucleus	igneous	vibrate	circuit
stomach	lava	erosion	digestion	crust

1. This can pour from a volcano.   — Ⓞ — —

2. This floats on the Earth's mantle.   Ⓞ — — — —

3. The esophagus leads to this.   — — Ⓞ — — —

4. One is small, the other is large.   — — — — — — — Ⓞ —

5. This feeds the cells of the body.   Ⓞ — — — — — — — —

6. Electric current flows through this.   — — — — Ⓞ — —

7. This directs cell activities.   — — Ⓞ — — — —

8. Plucked strings do this.   — — — — — Ⓞ —

9. This describes volcanic rock.   — — — — Ⓞ — —

10. This leads to soil in new places.   — Ⓞ — — — — —

Write the circled letters in order on the blanks. You will find the answer to this riddle. *How are an electric current and a group of musicians alike?*

Both need __   __ __ __ __ __ __ __ __ __.

Play With Words

If So, Then Write

Read the instructions. Then, write the correct letter on the blank. When you finish, you should have spelled a science word.

1. If lava comes from magma, write *E* on blank 1. If lava comes from fossils, write *T* on blank 1.

2. If veins and arteries are sedimentary, write *A* on blank 2. If veins and arteries are made of cells, write *X* on blank 2.

3. If faults occur on the Earth's crust, write *P* on blank 3. If faults are the result of weathering, write *N* on blank 3.

4. If electric current flows through an insulator, write *K* on blank 4. If electric current flows through a conductor, write *E* on blank 4.

5. If erosion is part of the rock cycle, write *R* on blank 5. If erosion has nothing to do with the rock cycle, write *G* on blank 5.

6. If a nucleus is made of tissues, write *O* on blank 6. If an organ is made of tissues, write *I* on blank 6.

7. If a wavelength has to do with how loud a sound is, write Y on blank 7. If a wavelength has to do with how high a sound is, write M on blank 7.

8. If a vibrating object has a circuit, write *B* on blank 8. If a vibrating object has a pitch, write *E* on blank 8.

9. If a volcano holds magma, write *N* on blank 9. If a volcano holds a fault, write *P* on blank 9.

10. If a nucleus is part of a cell, write *T* on blank 10. If a cell is part of a nucleus, write *S* on blank 10.

Important Technology Words You Need to Know!

Use this list to keep track of how well you know the new words.

0 = Don't Know   1 = Know It Somewhat   2 = Know It Well

___ ___ durable

___ ___ effort

___ ___ electronic

___ ___ friction

___ ___ fulcrum

___ ___ function

___ ___ gravity

___ ___ icon

___ ___ innovation

___ ___ lever

___ ___ load

___ ___ mechanical

___ ___ memory

___ ___ menu

___ ___ multimedia

___ ___ nonrenewable

___ ___ processor

___ ___ reliable

___ ___ renewable

___ ___ structure

Explore a Word

Follow these steps.

1. Read the paragraph below. Think about the meaning of the **bold** word.

> Technology is any process or thing that a person invents to solve a problem. Paper clips, bridges, and cellular phones are all technologies. An **innovation** to a technology makes it work better.

2. What do you think the word means? Write your idea.

   innovation: _____

   _____

3. Write a sentence with the word **innovation**. Show what it means.

   _____

   _____

4. Check the meaning of **innovation** in the Student Dictionary.

5. If your sentence in step 3 matches the meaning, put a ✓ after it. If your sentence does not match the meaning, write a better sentence.

   _____

   _____

6. Make a simple drawing to show the meaning of **innovation**.

Words Every Fourth Grader Needs to Know!

Explore a Word

Read the paragraph below. Think about the meaning of the **bold** word.

> The prefix *multi-* means "many." The word *media* means "more than one medium." A medium is a way of giving information or communicating with the public. **Multimedia** is a combination of text, sound, graphics, animations, photos, video, and other media. Multimedia is computer-controlled. Video games are one form of multimedia.

Complete the web to show your understanding of the word *multimedia.*

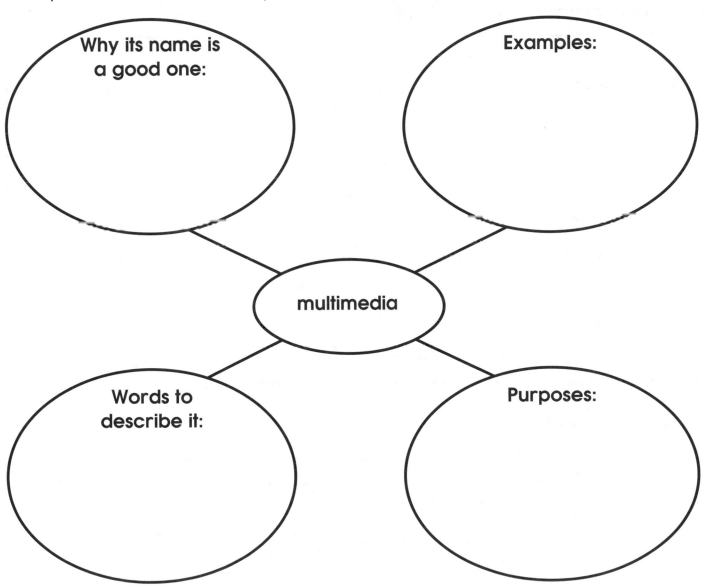

Why its name is a good one:

Examples:

multimedia

Words to describe it:

Purposes:

Compare Words

Name _____

Read the paragraph below. Think about the meaning of each **bold** word. Then, check the Student Dictionary.

> Engineers must ask themselves certain questions every time they design a new product. They ask, "Will this product work the same way every time we use it? Is it **reliable**?" They also ask, "Is this product made of materials that will last? Is it **durable**?"

Draw a picture of a product, such as a toothbrush, that you use every day. Write a caption telling why it is reliable. Then, write a caption explaining what makes it durable.

Word Alert!

A suffix is added to the end of a word or a root. It changes the word meaning or the way a word is used. The suffix -*able* means "able to be." Complete each sentence with your own idea.

1. When you rely on something, you depend on it. If something is reliable, it _____.

2. The root *dur* comes from a Latin word meaning "to last." If something is durable, it _____.

38

Words Every Fourth Grader Needs to Know!

Compare Words

Read the paragraph below. Think about the meaning of each **bold** word. Then, check the Student Dictionary.

> Engineers study the form and shape of things in nature. They learn about **structures** in the natural world, from plant fibers to birds' wings. They think about how each structure matches its **function** and does its job well. Then, they design their own structures to match functions.

Complete each sentence with your own idea.

1. The structure of a bridge is like the structure of a skeleton. Both a bridge and a skeleton have the function of _____

_____.

2. The function of an airplane's wing is like the function of a bird's wing. Both types of wings have a structure that _____

_____.

3. Engineers know that a tube is a strong structure. In the body, tubes such as blood vessels have the function of _____

_____.

4. The main function of an animal's fur is to keep the animal warm. People have used the structure of fur to design _____

_____.

Compare Words

Look at the pictures and captions. Think about the meaning of each **bold** word. Then, check the Student Dictionary.

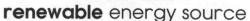

renewable energy source

nonrenewable energy source

Circle the word that completes each paragraph.

1. Much of our electric power is made by burning coal, oil, and natural gas. But these fossil fuels need millions of years to develop. The supplies will run out someday. Fossil fuels are (renewable, nonrenewable) sources of energy.

2. The Sun sends energy to the Earth in the forms of light and heat. People have learned how to use solar energy to make electric power. But the methods for using this (renewable, nonrenewable) source are costly.

3. In some parts of the world, hot magma reaches up through the Earth's crust. This heat from inside the Earth, or geothermal energy, can be turned into electric power. Geothermal energy is a (renewable, nonrenewable) source.

Word Alert!

The vocabulary words on this page are made up of prefixes and suffixes added to the same word. Look at the chart. Fill in the missing parts.

Prefix	Prefix	Word	Suffix	Long Word
	re- means "again"	1.	*-able* means "able to be"	*renewable* means "able to be made new again"
non- means "not"	2.	*new*	3.	4.

Compare Words

Read the paragraph below. Think about the meaning of each **bold** word. Then, check the Student Dictionary.

> A **mechanical** device, such as a washing machine, has moving parts. A mechanical device may be powered by electricity. Today, many machines also have **electronic** parts. These electronic parts use electric signals on tiny circuits.

Circle *Yes* or *No* for each question. Write your reason on the line.

1. Is an electric can opener a mechanical device? Yes No

_____

2. Does a cell phone have electronic parts? Yes No

_____

3. Is a television an electronic device? Yes No

_____

4. Is a laptop computer a mechanical invention? Yes No

_____

5. Were the first airplanes electronic? Yes No

_____

6. Can mechanical and electronic parts work together? Yes No

_____

Compare Words

Read the paragraph below. Think about the meaning of each **bold** word. Then, check the Student Dictionary.

> Imagine you are on your bike at the top of a hill. The force of **gravity** pulls you down the hill. Then, you're on flat ground. If you don't pedal, what will happen? The force of **friction** will cause your bike to slow down and come to a stop.

Read each description. Is it an example of gravity or friction? Circle the answer.

1. Things fall down, not up.

   (gravity)   friction

2. A rolling ball stops rolling.

   gravity   (friction)

3. Car tires grip the road without slipping.

   gravity   (friction)

4. The planets stay in orbit around the Sun.

   gravity   (friction)

5. Heavy birds flap their wings hard to get off the ground.

   (gravity)   friction

 Challenge!

Imagine jumping into a pool or lake. Picture walking through waist-high water. Use the words _friction_ and _gravity_ to describe what you imagine.

gravity pulled me down when I jump into the pool. And friction makes me slow down in the pool.

Words Every Fourth Grader Needs to Know!

Make Connections

Look at the diagram. Think about the meaning of each **bold** word. Then, check the Student Dictionary.

A seesaw is a simple machine called a **lever**.

The bar turns on the **fulcrum**.

The force of **effort** lifts the **load** at the other end.

Draw a picture. Show how you could use a lever to pry a heavy rock out of the ground. Write captions using the vocabulary words.

Make Connections

Read the paragraph below. Think about the meaning of each **bold** word. Then, check the Student Dictionary.

> Click on an **icon** on the computer desktop, and a program opens. Pull down a **menu**, and choose an action you want the program to perform. As you take these steps, the computer's **processors** are taking their own steps—at lightning speed! The processors are made of millions of tiny electronic switches that control electric circuits. The main processor is on a chip. Other chips hold **memory**, which is the data and instructions the processors use.

Complete each sentence. Include the vocabulary word in your answer.

1. menu
   When I want to print something, I _____

   _____.

2. processor
   A computer can't really think like a person, but _____

   _____.

3. icon
   If I want to open a program on my computer, I _____

   _____.

4. memory
   I can't play video games on this older computer, because _____

   _____.

Look It Up!

Computer terms are similar to everyday words. Look up the words *menu* and *memory* in a classroom dictionary. Answer each question below.

How is a computer menu like a restaurant menu? _____

_____

How is a person's memory like a computer's memory? _____

_____

Play With Words

Code Words

Choose the word that fits in each sentence. Circle its letter.

1. The job of a machine is its ___.
   - c mechanical
   - d processor
   - e function

2. A ___ encyclopedia has video clips.
   - n multimedia
   - o function
   - p mechanical

3. ___ is a force that slows motion.
   - f Electronic
   - g Friction
   - h Effort

4. An elbow joint is like ___.
   - i a fulcrum
   - j a load
   - k an innovation

5. A ___ is a simple machine.
   - l processor
   - m structure
   - n lever

6. A small picture on a screen is ___.
   - c durable
   - d multimedia
   - e an icon

7. ___ keeps our feet on the ground.
   - e Gravity
   - f Effort
   - g Innovation

8. Wind is a ___ source of energy.
   - q nonrenewable
   - r renewable
   - s gravity

Write the circled letters in order. You will find the name of a worker who creates technology.

_____

Play With Words

Synonym Mix-Up

Unscramble the letters to write a synonym for the vocabulary word.

1. structure   h e a p s   _____

2. innovation   e g a n c h   _____

3. nonrenewable   o n g e   _____

4. menu   s t i l   _____

5. fulcrum   t i v o p   _____

6. function   r u p p e s o   _____

7. icon   g e i m a   _____

8. durable   g h u o t   _____

Antonym Search

Find and circle the antonym for each word in the box. Look across and down.

renewable	reliable	durable	innovation

T	R	A	I	F	R	O	O	N	L	B
E	I	R	S	I	T	H	S	C	O	I
S	A	M	E	N	E	S	S	D	P	E
X	E	F	O	I	A	D	E	R	H	S
O	N	J	A	S	N	R	U	W	I	A
F	E	D	I	H	P	B	A	I	R	L
G	U	N	R	E	L	I	A	B	L	E
E	N	G	A	D	Q	U	K	O	T	L
W	N	K	R	F	L	I	M	S	Y	O
P	R	E	L	T	O	M	A	N	E	S

Important Language Arts Words You Need to Know!

Use this list to keep track of how well you know the new words.

0 = Don't Know   1 = Know It Somewhat   2 = Know It Well

___ 2 adjective
___ 2 adverb
___ 2 agreement
___ 2 apostrophe
___ 2 compare and contrast
___ 2 conjunction
___ 1 essay
___ 1 folktale
___ 2 idiom
___ 2 irregular plural
___ 2 metaphor
___ 2 mystery
___ 2 narrator
___ 2 outline
___ 1 persuade
___ 2 plot
___ 2 possession
___ 2 prefix

2 ___ pronoun
2 ___ punctuation
2 ___ research
1 ___ simile
2 ___ subject
2 ___ suffix
2 ___ summarize
2 ___ suspense
2 ___ thesaurus
2 ___ topic sentence
2 ___ trickster
2 ___ word origin

Explore a Word

Follow these steps.

1. Read the sentences below. Think about the meaning of the **bold** term.

> The pictures in the book help readers **compare and contrast** frogs and toads. These animals are alike in some ways and different in others.

2. What do you think the term means? Write your idea.

   compare and contrast: *that some things are the same in some ways and different in other ways.*

3. Write a sentence with the term **compare and contrast**. Show what it means.

   Toads and frogs are different because toads are bigger than frogs and toads have little bumps on their skin.

4. Check the meaning of **compare and contrast** in the Student Dictionary.

5. If your sentence in step 3 matches the meaning, put a ✓ after it. If your sentence does not match the meaning, write a better sentence.

   _____

   _____

6. Make a simple drawing to show the meaning of **compare and contrast**.

Words Every Fourth Grader Needs to Know!

Explore a Word

Read the sentence below. Think about the meaning of the **bold** word. Then, check the Student Dictionary.

> The students did **research** to find information about their city's history.

Complete the web to show your understanding of the word *research*.

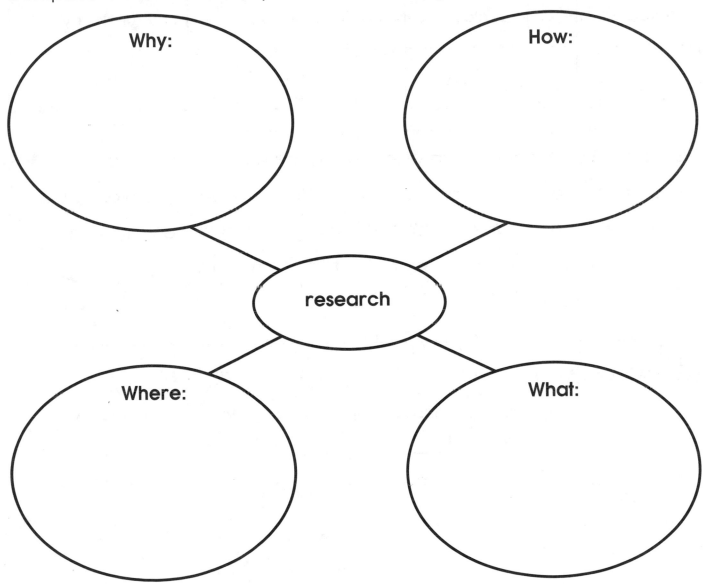

Why:

How:

research

Where:

What:

Compare Words

Look at the word equations below. Think about the meaning of each **bold** word. Then, check the Student Dictionary.

Prefix	+	Word	+	Suffix	=	New Word
re-	+	view	+	-er	=	reviewer
un-	+	clear	+	-ly	=	unclearly
dis-	+	agree	+	-able	=	disagreeable

Circle the word that completes each sentence.

1. In the word *agreement*, a (prefix/suffix) is added to the word *agree*.

2. In the word *disagree*, a (prefix/suffix) is added to the word *agree*.

3. The (prefix/suffix) *non-* means "not" in the word *nonsense*.

4. Add a (prefix/suffix) to the word *care* to make *careless* or *careful*.

5. The word *undo* has a (prefix/suffix).

 Word Alert!

The prefix *pre-* means "before" or "in front of." How does this help you to remember the meaning of the vocabulary word *prefix*?

_____

_____

Compare Words

Read the advice column below. Think about the meaning of each **bold** word. Then, check the Student Dictionary.

> Dear Student Writer:
>
> Make your writing interesting and clear by using sharp describing words. An **adjective** describes a person, place, or thing. You could use the adjective *good* to describe food. *The restaurant serves good food.* But what are some better, sharper adjectives to use instead? How about *spicy, fresh,* or *healthful*?
>
> An **adverb** is another describing word. It describes how something is done. In these sentences, the adverbs end with the suffix *-ly*. *We looked at the menu hungrily. We ordered quickly. We ate happily.* Remember to use adverbs wisely!
>
> Sincerely,
> Helpful Hinter

Follow each instruction.

1. Write three adjectives to describe today's weather.

_____

2. Write two adverbs to tell how someone spoke.

_____

3. Write two adjectives to describe the noun *tree*.

_____

4. Rewrite the sentence. Add one adjective and one adverb to make it more interesting.

The boys ate the pizza.

_____

Name _____

Make Connections

Read the sentences and examples below. Think about the meaning of each **bold** word. Then, check the Student Dictionary.

> A verb must agree with its **subject**. Check for subject-verb **agreement** in your sentences.
>
> If the subject is a singular noun or the **pronoun** *he*, *she*, or *it*, add –*s* to the verb.
>
> Example: Jack <u>helps</u> his mother. She <u>depends</u> on him.
> subject verb   subject   verb
>
> If the subject is a plural noun or the pronoun *I, we, you,* or *they*, do not add -*s* to the verb.
>
> Example: The friends <u>meet</u> at the park. They <u>play</u> every day.
> subject   verb   subject verb

Find the five errors in this paragraph. Fix each error. Add notes to the writer, explaining why the sentences need to be fixed. Use the vocabulary words in your notes.

○	My favorite color is green. It remind me of a forest of beautiful trees. Fresh green vegetables tastes great! A green, grassy lawn look like a welcome mat. I always wear something green. My parents drive a green car. We lives in a green house on Green Street. Green things just makes me smile!
○	

52

Make Connections

Read the sentences and examples. Think about the meaning of each **bold** word. Then, check the Student Dictionary.

A **simile** uses *like* or *as* to compare unlike things.	A **metaphor** compares unlike things directly.	An **idiom** is a saying in which the words don't have their usual meaning.
Example: Freddie can be <u>as stubborn as a bulldog</u>!	Example: When Freddie wants something, <u>he is a bulldog</u>!	Example: Someday, Freddie will <u>learn his lesson</u>!

Read each sentence. Underline the words that are a simile, a metaphor, or an idiom. Then, circle the correct description.

1. Gracie ran as fast as the wind.   simile   metaphor   idiom

2. The clouds are cotton balls.   simile   metaphor   idiom

3. She spoke in a voice like thunder!   simile   metaphor   idiom

4. Your answer is right on the button.   simile   metaphor   Idiom

5. The playroom is a trash dump.   simile   metaphor   idiom

6. It's raining cats and dogs!   simile   metaphor   idiom

 Challenge!

Choose one of the sentences above. Write another sentence that could come after it, telling more about the idea. Include a simile, a metaphor, or an idiom in your sentence.

_____

_____

Make Connections

Read the sentences below. Think about the meaning of each **bold** word. Then, check the Student Dictionary.

> The **narrator** begins the African **folktale** by saying, "This is a story about Ananse the Spider. Ananse is a **trickster** who sometimes gets tricked himself."

Circle *Yes* or *No* for each question. Write your reason on the line.

1. Are most folktales about tricksters?   Yes   No

   _____

2. Does a folktale always have a narrator?   Yes   No

   _____

3. Are most folktales old?   Yes   No

   _____

4. Is a trickster a generous character?   Yes   No

   _____

5. Is a trickster like a narrator?   Yes   No

   _____

6. Can a narrator be a story character?   Yes   No

   _____

Make Connections

Read the information below. Think about the meaning of each **bold** word. Then, check the Student Dictionary.

One mark of **punctuation** is called the **apostrophe**. Below are three rules for using an apostrophe with the letter *s* to show **possession**.

If the owner is a singular noun, use an apostrophe before the *s*.	If the owner is a plural noun, use the apostrophe after the *s*.	If the owner is an **irregular plural**, use the apostrophe before the *s*.
Examples: Emma's house, one boy's shirts	Examples: the girls' team, the friends' families	Examples: the children's room, the men's hats

Follow each instruction.

1. Write a sentence with two marks of punctuation.

   _____

   _____

2. Write a sentence about a girl with two pets. Use an apostrophe to show possession.

   _____

   _____

3. Write the irregular plurals of the words *mouse* and *woman*.

   _____

   _____

4. Write a sentence about the classrooms of three teachers. Use an apostrophe to show possession.

   _____

   _____

Make Connections

Read the paragraph below. Think about the meaning of each **bold** term. Then, check the Student Dictionary.

> Write an **essay** to **persuade** your readers to agree with you. Before you begin writing, make an **outline** as part of your planning step. As you draft, write a **topic sentence** for each paragraph.

Underline the better ending to each sentence.

1. A common way people try to persuade others is
   A. with advertising.
   B. by storytelling.

2. The purpose of a topic sentence is
   A. to prepare readers for a main idea.
   B. to plan what you will include in your writing.

3. An outline is like a list of
   A. books and other sources.
   B. the ideas in a written work.

4. An essay is a kind of written work that
   A. has a story problem, setting, and characters.
   B. shows the writer's knowledge and opinions.

5. An example of a topic sentence in an essay meant to persuade is:
   A. "Here are the steps in making buttery biscuits."
   B. "The school day should be an hour longer."

Make Connections

Read the paragraph below. Think about the meaning of each **bold** word. Then, check the Student Dictionary.

> If you like reading **mystery** stories filled with **suspense**, then I recommend reading *The Night Noises*. The **plot** begins when a boy discovers a buried treasure in the woods. I would **summarize** the rest of the story, but I don't want to give away the ending!

Circle *Yes* or *No* for each question. Write your reason on the line.

1. When you summarize, do you sum up what happened?   Yes   No

_____

2. Is the plot the same as the setting?   Yes   No

_____

3. Is suspense exciting?   Yes   No

_____

4. Is a mystery like a crime story?   Yes   No

_____

5. Is it possible to summarize a plot?   Yes   No

_____

 Look It Up!

Suspense can make you feel as if you are hanging in mid-air. Use a classroom dictionary to find the meaning of a related word, *suspend*. Explain how the meanings of the two words are related.

_____

_____

Make Connections

Read each pair of vocabulary words. Write the words where they fit in the sentences. Check the Student Dictionary for any meanings that you need.

I. thesaurus   adjective

Bella wanted to replace the _____ *nice* with a sharper word. She looked in the _____ for a list of synonyms. She chose the _____ *kindhearted*.

2. apostrophe   punctuation

The comma and the _____ are both marks of _____. They look alike, but the _____ is placed higher than the comma.

3. conjunction   adverb

In the phrase "bravely and boldly," the _____ *and* comes between the _____ *bravely* and the _____ *boldly*.

4. word origin   prefix

Look in a dictionary entry for information about a _____. The information may show how a _____ and a word root were joined long ago. A _____ shows how the word has changed over time.

5. subject   pronoun

An incorrect sentence is *My sister and me share a room.* The _____ *me* is the _____ of the sentence. The correct _____ is *I*.

6. similes   idioms

Poets use _____ to compare things in interesting ways. Speakers often use _____ without thinking about them. _____ are common in everyday speech.

Choose two of the vocabulary words on this page. Write them in a sentence.

_____

_____

Play With Words

Code Words

Choose the word that fits in each sentence. Circle its letter.

1. The word *happy* is an ___.
   r adverb
   s adjective
   t essay

2. A ___ begins with a problem.
   e plot
   f simile
   g narrator

3. The word *child* has an ___.
   l apostrophe
   m idiom
   n irregular plural

4. An apostrophe signals ___.
   t possession
   u pronouns
   v agreement

5. A folktale character might be a ___.
   c mystery
   d thesaurus
   e trickster

6. Introduce a paragraph with a ___.
   p conjunction
   n topic sentence
   r word origin

7. A subject must be ___ with its verb.
   h in suspense
   i in outline
   c in agreement

8. Can you ___ a metaphor and a simile?
   d research and persuade
   e compare and contrast
   f outline and summarize

Write the circled letters in order. You will find the place to use punctuation.

in a _____

Play With Words

Letter by Letter

Choose the word that fits with each clue. Write it letter by letter. Some letters will be inside circles.

conjunction	folktale	outline	research	thesaurus
essay	metaphor	pronoun	suffix	

1. -ly, -ness, -ful   __ ◯ __ __ __ __

2. I, me, he, them   __ __ ◯ __ __ __

3. and, or, but   ◯ __ __ __ __ __ __ __ __ __ __

4. *The Little Red Hen*   __ __ __ __ __ ◯ __ __

5. Full of synonyms   __ __ ◯ __ __ __ __ __ __

6. A way to find information   __ __ __ ◯ __ __ __ __

7. The phrase "A book is a treasure."   __ __ __ __ __ __ __ ◯

8. Lists topics, subtopics, details   __ __ __ ◯ __ __ __

9. A writing on a topic   __ __ __ __ ◯

Write the circled letters in order on the blanks. You will find the answer to this question. *What word do students always pronounce unclearly?*

__ __ __ __ __ __ __ __ __ __

Important History Words You Need to Know!

Use this list to keep track of how well you know the new words.

0 = Don't Know   1 = Know It Somewhat   2 = Know It Well

___ ___ agriculture

___ ___ ally

___ ___ ancestor

___ ___ conflict

___ ___ debate

___ ___ equality

___ ___ folklore

___ ___ found

___ ___ frontier

___ ___ game

___ ___ generation

___ ___ hardship

___ ___ heritage

___ ___ hunter-gatherers

___ ___ independence

___ ___ inhabitant

___ ___ integration

___ ___ international

___ ___ irrigation

___ ___ Loyalist

___ ___ migration

___ ___ militia

___ ___ national

___ ___ nomadic

___ ___ Patriot

___ ___ pioneer

___ ___ primary source

___ ___ protest

___ ___ rituals

___ ___ secondary source

___ ___ segregation

___ ___ statehood

___ ___ territory

___ ___ tradition

___ ___ treaty

Explore a Word

Follow these steps.

1. Read the sentences below. Think about the meaning of the **bold** word.

> The American colonies fought a war for **independence** from Britain.

2. What do you think the word means? Write your idea.

   independence: _____

   _____

3. Write a sentence with the word **independence**. Show what it means.

   _____

   _____

4. Check the meaning of **independence** in the Student Dictionary.

5. If your sentence in step 3 matches the meaning, put a ✓ after it. If your sentence does not match the meaning, write a better sentence.

   _____

   _____

6. Make a simple drawing to show the meaning of **independence**.

Explore a Word

Read the sentences below. Think about the meaning of each **bold** word. Then, check the Student Dictionary.

> If nations cannot settle their differences peacefully, the result is **conflict**.
>
> Travelers faced many **hardships** as they crossed the desert. Lack of water was one of the big problems.

Fill in the missing parts of the charts to show your understanding of the words *conflict* and *hardship*.

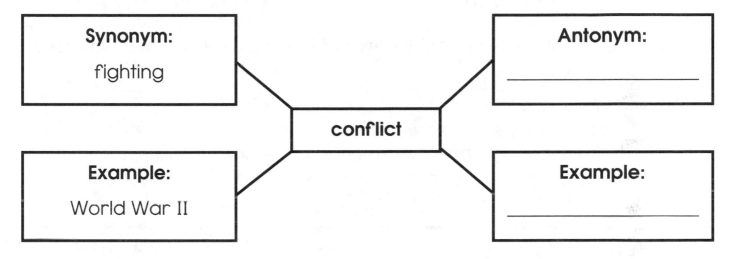

Synonym: fighting

Antonym: _____

conflict

Example: World War II

Example: _____

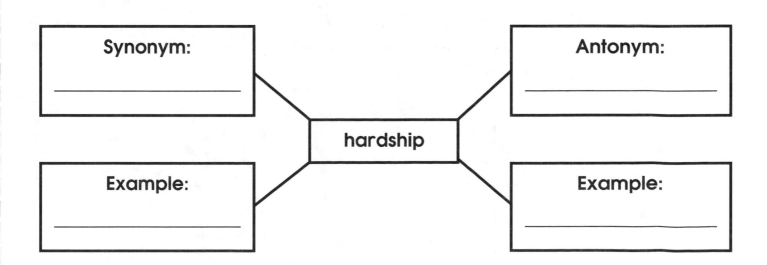

Synonym: _____

Antonym: _____

hardship

Example: _____

Example: _____

Compare Words

Look at the pictures and captions. Think about the meaning of each **bold** term. Then, check the Student Dictionary.

primary source

secondary source

Read the questions. Use your answers to fill in the chart. Then, add more details to the chart.

What can you learn from both kinds of sources?
When are secondary sources written?
Why do historians study primary sources?
What kind of source is a president's speech? a history textbook? an encyclopedia? an eyewitness account?

Primary Source	Both	Secondary Source

Words Every Fourth Grader Needs to Know!

Compare Words

Read the paragraph below. Think about the meaning of each **bold** word. Then, check the Student Dictionary.

> Britain ruled the American colonies. Some colonists were **Loyalists** and felt strong ties to Britain. Other colonists dreamed of a separate American nation. They were known as **Patriots**.

Circle the word that completes each sentence.

1. American colonists who fought against Britain were called (Patriots/Loyalists).

2. American colonists who sided with Britain were (Patriots/Loyalists).

3. The (Patriots/Loyalists) wanted to obey the laws of Britain.

4. The (Patriots/Loyalists) wanted independence for the colonies.

5. The (Patriots/Loyalists) won the American Revolution.

Word Alert!

Words that belong to the same word family have related meanings. Complete the sentences with words from the box.

patriot	patriotism	loyalty
patriotic	loyal	loyally

1. A _____ loves his or her country. Saluting the flag is a sign of _____. Defending one's country is a _____ act.

2. People can be _____ to a leader. They show their _____ by giving steady support. They speak and act _____.

Compare Words

Read the sentences below. Think about the meaning of each **bold** word. Then, check the Student Dictionary.

> The **national** news report told about Louisiana and Texas. The **international** news report told about China and Japan.

Circle the word that completes each sentence.

1. Trucks drive from Florida to California on (national/international) highways.

2. Trade among countries is (national/international).

3. America's (national/international) anthem is the "Star-Spangled Banner."

4. There are (national/international) laws protecting the world's oceans.

5. Athletes from many lands compete in (national/international) games.

Word Alert!

A prefix is a word part added before a word. A suffix is a word part added to the end of a word. Prefixes and suffixes change word meaning.

Prefix	Word	Suffix	Meaning
inter- means "between"	*nation*	*-al* makes a describing word	*international* means "involving two or more nations"

Put these word parts together to write one longer word.

inter-	-al	continent

Can you say a sentence with the longer word?

Make Connections

Read the paragraph below. Think about the meaning of each **bold** term. Then, check the Student Dictionary.

> Early people lived as **hunter-gatherers**. They ate roots, seeds, and other wild plants that they gathered. They hunted **game** for food. Many groups were **nomadic** and followed the animals they hunted. This way of life changed when **agriculture** began and farming settlements grew.

Circle *Yes* or *No* for each question. Write your reason on the line.

1. Do nomadic people build large cities?   Yes   No

    _____

2. Are most hunter-gatherers also farmers?   Yes   No

    _____

3. Is agriculture the same as farming?   Yes   No

    _____

4. Is corn an example of game?   Yes   No

    _____

5. Are hunter-gatherers nomadic?   Yes   No

    _____

 Look It Up!

Each meaning of a word is numbered in a dictionary entry. Look up the word *game* in a classroom dictionary. Write the meaning that fits with this page.

_____

Make Connections

ancestor	generation	heritage	folklore	rituals

Check the Student Dictionary for the meaning of each vocabulary word in the box. Read each set of listed things. Think about why they belong together. Then, write the vocabulary word that names the category.

1. _____

   wedding ceremonies
   forms of worship
   holiday parades

2. _____

   a group of cousins
   a period of about 30 years
   parents, uncles, and aunt

3. _____

   Grandmother's grandfather
   a relative from long ago
   a great-great-great grandparent

4. _____

   tall tales
   nursery rhymes
   songs of long ago

5. _____

   something passed down through time
   beliefs shared with people who came before you
   a connection with the past

 Challenge!

Write one interesting sentence using three of the vocabulary words.

_____

_____

Words Every Fourth Grader Needs to Know!

Make Connections

protest	debate	equality	segregation	integration

Check the Student Dictionary for the meaning of each vocabulary word in the box. Read the paragraphs. Write the vocabulary words that could replace the **bold** words.

1. Until the 1950s, African-American children in Southern states could not go to schools with white children. State laws required the **separation** of people based on race.

   _____

2. African Americans did not have the same chance for education that white people had. They did not have the same chance for jobs. Leaders stepped forward to fight for **balanced chances** for all people.

   _____

3. One of the leaders was Martin Luther King, Jr. He believed that people should **object to** unfair laws in peaceful ways.

   _____

4. Martin Luther King, Jr. helped organize marches. Thousands of people marched to support the **opening to all people** of public schools, buildings, and other places.

   _____

5. The **argument** about civil rights is an important part of American history.

   _____

 Challenge!

Write one sentence using the words *integration* and *segregation*.

_____

_____

Make Connections

Read the paragraph below. Think about the meaning of each **bold** word. Then, check the Student Dictionary.

> The **frontier** of the United States kept moving westward. **Pioneers** cleared forests, built cabins, and began farming. They founded new communities. Areas with just a few **inhabitants** grew into thriving towns.

Circle *Yes* or *No* for each question. Write your reason on the line.

1. A group wanted to found a settlement. Had they lost it?   Yes   No

   _____

2. Is a frontier a kind of place?   Yes   No

   _____

3. Does an inhabitant usually live in a wild land?   Yes   No

   _____

4. Is a pioneer like an explorer?   Yes   No

   _____

5. Could a pioneer be an inhabitant?   Yes   No

   _____

 Look It Up!

Some words that look alike come from different origins. These words have separately numbered entries in a dictionary. Look up the word *found* in a classroom dictionary. Write the meaning that fits with each word.

1. The city was founded in 1700.

   _____

2. Have you found the city on the map?

   _____

Make Connections

Read each pair of vocabulary words. Write the words where they fit in the sentences. Check the Student Dictionary for any meanings that you need.

1. ally   treaty

   Each nation's leaders signed the _____. Each nation promised to be a helpful _____ to the others.

2. agriculture   irrigation

   Plants need water, so farmers have always used methods of _____. Managing soil and insect pests are also important in _____.

3. migration   frontier

   The western _____ called to Americans seeking new homes. The _____ westward was part of American history.

4. tradition   generation

   The _____ of a Thanksgiving feast began long ago and has been passed down to each _____.

5. territory   statehood

   Arizona became a U.S. _____ in the 1800s and was granted _____ in 1912.

6. militia   Patriots

   The _____ asked each town for men to serve in a _____ to fight the British.

Now, choose two of the vocabulary words on this page. Write them in a sentence.

_____

_____

Make Connections

Read the paragraphs below. Think about the meaning of each **bold** word. Then, rewrite each paragraph using your own words. Do not use the vocabulary words in your sentences.

1. The **heritage** of Americans includes **folklore**. Each **generation** learns **traditional** stories about **frontier** heroes, such as Paul Bunyan and Johnny Appleseed.

   _____

   _____

   _____

   _____

2. The Native-American **inhabitants** of North America lived in every region. Some of them were **hunter-gatherers**. Others depended on agriculture. Some groups were **allies**, and others had conflicts.

   _____

   _____

   _____

   _____

3. Americans celebrate the **founding** of their country and **independence** from Britain as a **national** holiday. On July 4, Americans remember **Patriots** like George Washington and enjoy **traditions** like picnics and fireworks.

   _____

   _____

   _____

   _____

   _____

Play With Words

Letter by Letter

Choose the word that fits with each clue. Write it letter by letter. Some letters will be inside circles.

ancestor	hardship	statehood	segregation	militia
heritage	treaty	conflict	equality	protest

1. Hawaii was the 50th to get this. __ __ __ __ __ __ __ __ (○)

2. This kept groups apart. __ __ __ __ __ __ __ __ (○) __ __

3. Grandpa's grandma. __ __ (○) __ __ __ __ __

4. This is not a regular army. __ __ __ __ (○) __ __

5. This comes from the past. __ __ __ (○) __ __ __ __

6. This is a way of saying no. __ __ __ (○) __ __ __

7. War is one example. __ __ (○) __ __ __ __ __

8. This is an agreement. __ __ __ (○) __ __

9. Hunger is one example. __ __ (○) __ __ __ __ __

10. This is fair treatment. __ __ __ __ __ __ __ (○)

Write the circled letters in order on the blanks. You will find the answer to this question. *Where does Friday come before Thursday?*

in a __ __ __ __ __ __ __ __ __ __

Play With Words

Synonym Pairs

Read the clue. Find and circle the two synonyms that match the clue.

1. Sign this to make a promise.

   i f t r e a t y a j a g r e e m e n t o b i s

2. Without this, we don't eat.

   w o f a r m i n g r t h a g r i c u l t u r e d o

3. This is a loyal friend.

   i n p a r t n e r g i a l l y

4. Make your views known with this.

   t s d e b a t e w o a r g u m e n t r t h

5. This person goes first.

   d o s c o u t i n p i o n e e r g w

6. This is passed down through time.

   e l l t r a d i t i o n a s h e r i t a g e a y

7. Everyone wants to be treated with this.

   i n g e q u a l i t y f r o f a i r n e s s m f

8. This is movement to a new place.

   o l m i g r a t i o n k l j o u r n e y o r e

Look back to find the letters you did NOT circle. Write them in order on the lines below to find a message.

— — __ __ — — __ — — __ — — — — —

— — — — — , __ — — '— __ — — — — __

— — — — — __ — — — —!

—_ __ — — — — — __ — — — __

— — — — — — — — __

Play With Words

Synonym Mix-Up

Unscramble the letters to write a synonym for the vocabulary word.

1. independence   r d e f e m o   _____

2. territory   r g o i e n   _____

3. found   r c a e t e   _____

4. international   b l g o a l   _____

5. conflict   t t b l a e   _____

6. tradition   s t u m o c   _____

7. debate   c u d i s s s   _____

8. nomadic   m o a r i n g   _____

Antonym Search

Find and circle the antonym for each word in the box. Look across and down.

integration	equality	protest	ally	Patriot	hardship

```
I S T U V M I L L O W E
R I G H S D E B Q U A D
E L M I E A P P R O V E
G O I R G U E N P N T A
C A Y K R I N W A I E S
D I F F E R E N C E F E
A L E N G C M Y H X E V
S M B L A P Y D O B W D
J U M T T I A E Z G K H
R I G N I L R A Y V I G
D E N L O Y A L I S T R
P R E I T T O O X A M F
```

Play With Words

Code Words

Choose the word that fits in each sentence. Circle its letter.

1. Newcomers settled in the ___.
   - **g** migration
   - **h** territory
   - **i** inhabitant

2. ___ traveled west in wagon trains.
   - **i** Pioneers
   - **j** Militia
   - **k** Loyalists

3. Was the nation an enemy or an ___?
   - **q** international
   - **r** equality
   - **s** ally

4. All over the world, people perform religious ___.
   - **t** rituals
   - **u** conflict
   - **v** ancestor

5. In dry areas, crops need ___.
   - **n** agriculture
   - **o** irrigation
   - **p** hunter-gatherers

6. Cousins belong to the same ___.
   - **p** primary sources
   - **q** integration
   - **r** generation

7. Stories and songs from long ago are ___.
   - **h** secondary sources
   - **i** folklore
   - **j** national

8. Native Americans were the first ___ of Ohio.
   - **a** Patriots
   - **b** frontier
   - **c** inhabitants

Write the circled letters in order. You will find a word to describe an important event.

_____

Important Geography Words You Need to Know!

Use this list to keep track of how well you know the new words.

0 = Don't Know   1 = Know It Somewhat   2 = Know It Well

___ ___ adapt

___ ___ Antarctic

___ ___ Arctic

___ ___ biome

___ ___ canyon

___ ___ compass rose

___ ___ conservation

___ ___ delta

___ ___ drought

___ ___ equator

___ ___ floodplain

___ ___ glacier

___ ___ hemisphere

___ ___ latitude

___ ___ longitude

___ ___ physical feature

___ ___ plateau

___ ___ population

___ ___ region

___ ___ strait

___ ___ swamp

___ ___ tropics

___ ___ tundra

___ ___ vegetation

___ ___ wetland

Explore a Word

Follow these steps.

1. Read the paragraph below. Think about the meaning of the **bold** word.

> Some of the natural **regions** on the Earth include rain forests, deserts, and grasslands. A region can be made of people, too. Groups in the same cultural region usually speak the same language and share the same ways of life.

2. What do you think the word means? Write your idea.

   region: _____

   _____

3. Write a sentence with the word **region**. Show what it means.

   _____

   _____

4. Check the meaning of **region** in the Student Dictionary.

5. If your sentence in step 3 matches the meaning, put a ✓ after it. If your sentence does not match the meaning, write a better sentence.

   _____

   _____

6. Make a simple drawing to show the meaning of **region**.

Words Every Fourth Grader Needs to Know!

Explore a Word

Read the sentence below. Think about the meaning of each **bold** word. Then, check the Student Dictionary.

> The lake dried up during the long **drought**, and the surrounding **vegetation** turned brown and died.

Fill in the chart to show your understanding of each word.

	Drought	Vegetation
What Is It?		
What I Picture...		
Why Is It Important?		

Compare Words

Name _____

Look at the picture and captions. Think about the meaning of each **bold** word. Then, check the Student Dictionary.

The **Arctic** has the North Pole at its center. Native people of this region hunt and fish for food.

The **Antarctic** includes the southernmost continent of Antarctica. The few people who live there are scientists.

Circle the word that completes each sentence.

1. The (Arctic, Antarctic) includes the South Pole.

2. The Inuit are native people of the (Arctic, Antarctic).

3. Penguins of the southern oceans come ashore in the (Arctic, Antarctic).

4. Summer at the North Pole is winter in the (Arctic, Antarctic).

5. The northern parts of Canada are in the (Arctic, Antarctic).

 Look It Up!

The word *Arctic* can be an adjective that describes a noun. For example, *Arctic region*, *Arctic mammals*, and *Arctic people*. The word *arctic*, spelled with a lowercase *a*, is also an adjective. Look up *arctic* in a classroom dictionary. Use it to describe three nouns below.

_____

_____

_____

Compare Words

Look at the picture and caption. Think about the meaning of each **bold** word. Then, check the Student Dictionary.

The **equator** is an imaginary line that cuts the Earth in half. One **hemisphere** is north of the equator, and the other is south of it.

Circle *Yes* or *No* for each question. Write your reason on the line.

1. Is the Arctic in the Southern Hemisphere?   Yes   No

_____

2. Is a hemisphere half of the globe?   Yes   No

_____

3. Is it possible to step across the equator?   Yes   No

_____

4. Does the equator cross Antarctica?   Yes   No

_____

5. Could a country be in two hemispheres?   Yes   No

_____

6. Is the United States north of the equator?   Yes   No

_____

Make Connections

Look at the map and caption. Think about the meaning of each **bold** term. Then, check the Student Dictionary.

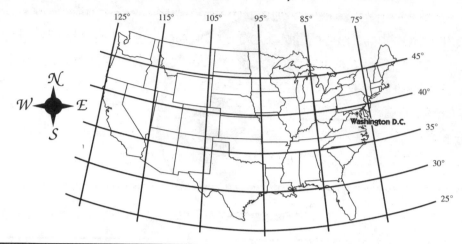

Lines of **latitude** go east-west. Lines of **longitude** go north-south.
A **compass rose** shows direction.

Use the vocabulary words to complete the paragraphs. Use each word twice.

Where in the world is your town? To find the answer, look on a map. The (1.) _____ points north. Is your town in the eastern or western part of your state? The (2.) _____ will help you find those directions.

Where, exactly, is the capital of the United States? Maps have lines that help you find locations. (3.) _____ is measured in degrees north or south of the equator. (4.) _____ is measured in degrees east or west of an imaginary line that runs north-south through England. Washington, D.C., has a (5.) _____ of 38° N. Its (6.) _____ is 77° W.

Make Connections

Read the paragraph. Think about the meaning of each **bold** term. Then, check the Student Dictionary.

> We began our trip by riding a ferry across the **strait**. Then, we took a bus to view a giant **glacier**. We walked across its icy surface! After that, we rode on a train across a **plateau**. When the flat land ended, the train dipped down. At last, we drove to a **canyon**. We peered down its steep walls. During the ride back, I circled all of these **physical features** on my map.

Complete each sentence with information about geography. Include the vocabulary word in your answer.

1. glaciers
   The Great Lakes formed during the last ice age, when _____

   _____.

2. physical features
   Maps show rivers, mountains, _____

   _____.

3. canyon
   A valley is a low area of land, but _____

   _____.

4. plateau
   A hill often has a round top, but _____

   _____.

5. strait
   Ships sailing from the lake to the bay must _____

   _____.

Make Connections

Read the paragraph below. Think about the meaning of each **bold** word. Then, check the Student Dictionary.

> People have **adapted** to every **biome** in the world. They have learned to live in the freezing **tundra**, the humid **tropics**, and the driest deserts. The world's human **population** is higher now than ever before.

Underline the better ending to each sentence.

1. People of the tundra depended on animals for food because
   A. the soil did not support crops.
   B. animals were easy to find.

2. A biome covers a large area in which
   A. there are similar kinds of plants and animals.
   B. the weather conditions are harsh.

3. Lands in the tropics generally have
   A. long winters and short summers.
   B. warm or hot temperatures all year.

4. The population of a region always
   A. grows larger.
   B. changes over time

5. People have learned to adapt to
   A. lands with different climates and vegetation.
   B. homes, clothing, and methods of finding food.

 Word Alert!

Words that belong to the same word family have related meanings. Write a sentence that contains the three words from the box.

adapted	adaptable	adaptation

_____

_____

Words Every Fourth Grader Needs to Know!

Make Connections

Read the paragraph below. Think about the meaning of each **bold** word. Then, check the Student Dictionary.

> The **conservation** of **wetlands** is important. For example, a **swamp** helps filter water and refill underground water supplies. Swamps often develop in the **floodplains** of a river. The river creates valuable wetlands in its **delta**, as it empties into the sea.

Complete each sentence with a word or phrase that makes sense.

1. People work on conservation projects in order to
_____ land, water, and life.

2. A swamp is a home to trees that can _____ in water.

3. A delta often has rich soil that the river _____.

4. A floodplain is a land that stretches on both sides of _____.

5. A wetland is valuable because it helps protect _____.

 Word Alert!

Two words put together are called a *compound word*. Two of the vocabulary words are compound words. Write a meaning for each compound word. Include both of the smaller words in your meaning.

_____

_____

_____

_____

Make Connections

Read each pair of vocabulary words. Write the words where they fit in the sentences. Check the Student Dictionary for any meanings that you need.

1. adapt   Antarctic

   Which sea mammals are able to _____ to the cold

   waters of the _____?

2. drought   population

   The _____ of the region suffered during the long

   _____.

3. tropics   equator

   The regions on either side of the _____ are called the

   _____.

4. glaciers   latitudes

   Today, _____ are found only in the _____

   near the North and South Poles.

5. biome   vegetation

   Similar kinds of _____ grow throughout a

   _____.

6. floodplain   conservation

   To protect the water supply, we need _____ of the

   _____.

Choose two of the vocabulary words on this page. Write them in a sentence. Then, write the sentence again on another sheet of paper. Leave blank lines for the two words. Challenge a partner to complete your sentence.

_____

_____

Make Connections

Read each list of vocabulary words. Cross out the word that does not fit with the others. Explain why this word does not belong. Check the Student Dictionary for any meanings that you need.

1. tundra, Arctic, glacier, swamp

   _____

2. compass rose, adapt, equator, physical feature

   _____

3. plateau, wetland, hemisphere, canyon

   _____

4. floodplain, biome, region, vegetation

   _____

5. strait, drought, delta, swamp

   _____

6. latitude, longitude, compass rose, conservation

   _____

 Challenge!

Look back at the three words that are left in each list. Add another word that belongs with them.

Play With Words

If So, Then Write

Read the instructions. Then, write the correct letter on the blank. When you finish, you should have spelled a geography word.

$$\overline{\rule{1em}{0.4pt}}\ \overline{\rule{1em}{0.4pt}}\ \overline{\rule{1em}{0.4pt}}\ \overline{\rule{1em}{0.4pt}}\ \overline{\rule{1em}{0.4pt}}\ \overline{\rule{1em}{0.4pt}}\ \overline{\rule{1em}{0.4pt}}\ \overline{\rule{1em}{0.4pt}}\ \overline{\rule{1em}{0.4pt}}\ \overline{\rule{1em}{0.4pt}}$$
1   2   3   4   5   6   7   8   9   10

1. If lines of latitude cross north and south, write *P* on blank 1. If lines of latitude cross east and west, write *C* on blank 1.

2. If a hemisphere is exactly half of the globe, write *O* on blank 2. If a hemisphere is less than half of the globe, write *L* on blank 2.

3. If there are glaciers in the Arctic, write *N* on blank 3. If there are no glaciers in the Arctic, write *T* on blank 3.

4. If a drought is good for farmers, write *S* on blank 4. If a drought is not good for farmers, write *T* on blank 4.

5. If a population has to do with people, write *I* on blank 5. If a population has nothing to do with people, write *E* on blank 5.

6. If vegetation includes only plants eaten as food, write *A* on blank 6. If vegetation includes all plants, write *N* on blank 6.

7. If a strait is narrow, write *E* on blank 7. If a strait is wide, write *O* on blank 7.

8. If a line of longitude crosses the Antarctic, write *N* on blank 8. If a line of longitude doesn't cross the Antarctic, write *M* on blank 8.

9. If a compass rose is a physical feature, write *R* on blank 9. If a canyon is a physical feature, write *T* on blank 9.

10. If the tundra is a biome, write *S* on blank 10. If the tundra is a plateau, write *O* on blank 10.

Play With Words

Code Words

Choose the word that fits in each sentence. Circle its letter.

1. A ___ is like a river of ice.
   - l delta
   - m glacier
   - n strait

2. A tropical rain forest is a ___.
   - m swamp
   - n drought
   - o biome

3. ___ lines are imaginary.
   - u Longitude
   - v Glacier
   - w Canyon

4. The North Pole is in the ___.
   - l equator
   - m Antarctic
   - n Arctic

5. High, flat land is a ___.
   - t plateau
   - u canyon
   - v floodplain

6. Cities have a high ___.
   - a population
   - b hemisphere
   - c conservation

7. A line of ___ runs north-south.
   - h latitude
   - i longitude
   - j equator

8. The ___ on a map points north.
   - m equator
   - n compass rose
   - o strait

Write the circled letters in order. You will find the name of a physical feature.

_____

Play With Words

Letter by Letter

Choose the word that fits with each clue. Write it letter by letter. Some letters will be inside circles.

vegetation	delta	swamp	floodplain	hemisphere
tropics	tundra	equator	drought	

1. A long time without rain   __ __ __ __ __ Ⓞ __

2. V-shaped land at river's mouth   __ __ __ __ Ⓞ

3. Trees, shrubs, grass, and more

   Ⓞ __ __ __ __ __ __ __ __ __

4. Line at 0° latitude   Ⓞ __ __ __ __ __ __

5. Florida's Everglades   __ __ __ __ Ⓞ

6. Where polar bears live   __ __ __ __ __ Ⓞ

7. Land along a river   __ __ __ __ __ __ Ⓞ __ __ __

8. Half the globe   __ __ Ⓞ __ __ __ __ __ __ __

9. Where rain forests grow   __ __ __ __ __ __ Ⓞ

Write the circled letters in order on the blanks to find the answer to this riddle. *How are your hands like a tropical region?*

Both __ __ __ __   __ __ __ __ __ __.

Important Civics and Economics Words You Need to Know!

Use this list to keep track of how well you know the new words.

0 = Don't Know   1 = Know It Somewhat   2 = Know It Well

___ ___ amendment

___ ___ Bill of Rights

___ ___ branches of government

___ ___ capital resources

___ ___ census

___ ___ Constitution

___ ___ demand

___ ___ executive

___ ___ human resources

___ ___ industry

___ ___ judicial

___ ___ jury

___ ___ labor

___ ___ legislative

___ ___ natural resources

___ ___ production

___ ___ representation

___ ___ suffrage

___ ___ supply

___ ___ taxation

Explore a Word

Follow these steps.

I. Read the sentences below. Think about the meaning of the **bold** word.

> The island nation had no mining **industry**, few factories, and a small fishing industry. Its main source of wealth was the tourism industry.

2. What do you think the word means? Write your idea.

industry: _____

_____

3. Write a sentence with the word **industry**. Show what it means.

_____

_____

4. Check the meaning of **industry** in the Student Dictionary.

5. If your sentence in step 3 matches the meaning, put a ✓ after it. If your sentence does not match the meaning, write a better sentence.

_____

_____

6. Make a simple drawing to show the meaning of **industry**.

Words Every Fourth Grader Needs to Know!

Explore a Word

Read the sentences below. Think about the meaning of the **bold** word. Then, check the Student Dictionary.

> People and businesses pay money to the government in various ways. Sales tax is one form of **taxation**. Income tax and property tax are others.

Fill out the web to show your ideas about taxation.

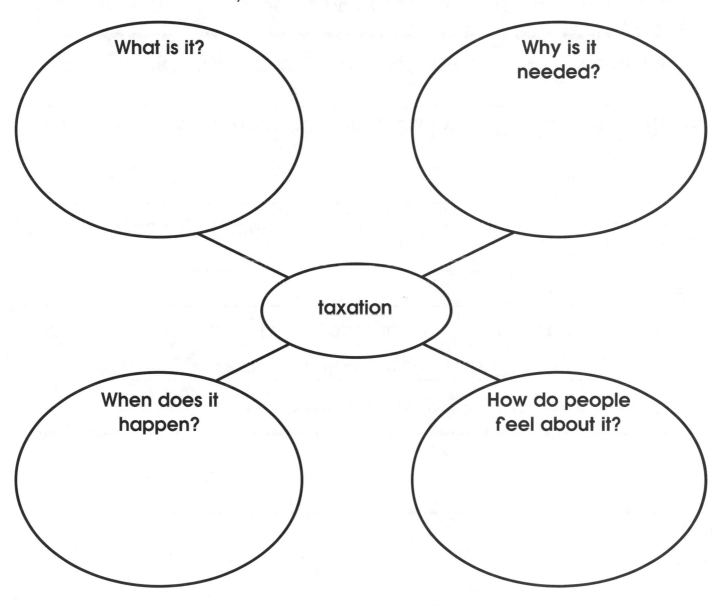

What is it?

Why is it needed?

taxation

When does it happen?

How do people feel about it?

Compare Words

Read the paragraph. Think about the meaning of each **bold** word. Then, check the Student Dictionary.

> How much does something cost? The price depends on **supply** and **demand**. Supply is the amount of a product that sellers are willing and able to sell at various prices. The demand is the amount of the product that buyers are willing and able to buy at various prices. When supply and demand are in balance, the price is right for both sellers and buyers.

Complete each sentence with your own ideas about supply, demand, and price.

1. The new gadget is so popular that stores have run out of them. The

   supply _____

   _____.

2. Max opened a lemonade stand and charged $10 for each cup. The

   demand _____

   _____.

3. It was a stormy season, and orange growers lost a lot of their crop. The price of oranges is high because the supply _____

   _____.

4. Your favorite breakfast cereal just doubled in price! Demand may

   _____

   _____.

Make Connections

Read the paragraph. Think about the meaning of each **bold** word. Then, check the Student Dictionary.

> **Suffrage** is valuable. The right to vote gives citizens a say in how they are governed. In the United States, voters in each state have **representation** in two main ways. They elect two lawmakers to the Senate. They also elect lawmakers to the House of Representatives. The number of Representatives depends on the state's population, which is based on a **census** taken every ten years.

Underline the better ending to each sentence.

1. The United States census gives information about
   A. who will represent citizens.
   B. who lives in the United States.

2. U.S. citizens have representation in
   A. the Senate and the House of Representatives.
   B. the House of Representatives.

3. Before women gained suffrage, they
   A. could not vote.
   B. had representation.

4. Suffrage has been granted to
   A. all U.S. citizens of voting age.
   B. the whole population.

5. Representation matters to citizens because
   A. they demand a census every ten years.
   B. they want lawmakers to serve them.

Make Connections

Read the paragraph below. Think about the meaning of each **bold** term. Then, check the Student Dictionary.

> The **Bill of Rights** is the name of the first ten **amendments** to the **Constitution** of the United States. Amendments five through eight protect the rights of people accused of crimes. This includes the right to a speedy and public trial by a **jury**.

Complete each sentence with one or two words that make sense.

1. The founders of the United States wrote the Constitution to _____ a government.

2. The Constitution explains how to make amendments that will _____ the law of the land.

3. The Bill of Rights limits _____ over people's freedom.

4. A jury is made of citizens who are expected to _____.

5. The first Amendment protects basic freedoms, such as the right to practice one's religion and the right to _____ in speech and print.

 Look It Up!

What is the difference between a constitution and the Constitution? Use a classroom dictionary to find the meaning of each word. Then, write a sentence to explain the difference.

_____

_____

Make Connections

Look at the chart. Think about the meaning of each **bold** term. Then, check the Student Dictionary.

The United States has three **branches of government**.

executive	**legislative**	**judicial**
President, Vice President, agencies and departments	U.S. Congress: Senate, House of Representatives	Supreme Court, system of federal courts

Use the vocabulary words from the captions to complete the paragraphs. Some words will be used twice.

The word *execute* can mean "to carry out" or "to put into action." The [1.] _____ branch carries out laws, making sure that they are obeyed. The laws are written by members of the [2.] _____ branch. Judgments about the laws are made by the [3.] _____ branch.

Each of these [4.] _____ can limit the power of the others. For example, the [5.] _____ branch appoints federal court judges. But the President's choices must be approved by lawmakers in the [6.] _____ branch. The judges in the [7.] _____ branch, in turn, can decide that actions taken by the President or Congress are not permitted by the U.S. Constitution.

Make Connections

Look at the chart. Think about the meaning of each **bold** term. Then, check the Student Dictionary.

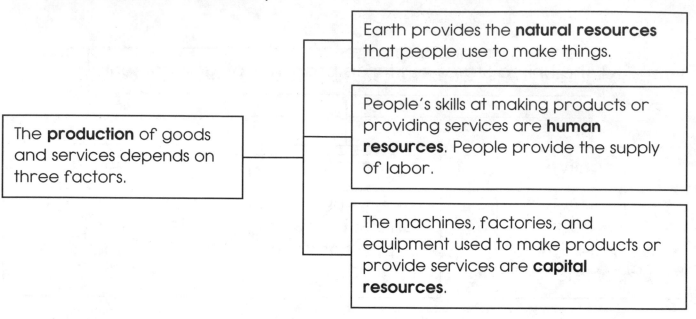

The **production** of goods and services depends on three factors.

Earth provides the **natural resources** that people use to make things.

People's skills at making products or providing services are **human resources**. People provide the supply of labor.

The machines, factories, and equipment used to make products or provide services are **capital resources**.

Circle *Yes* or *No* for each question. Write your reason on the line.

1. Is labor needed for production?   Yes   No

_____

2. Is a carpenter's hammer an example of a natural resource? Yes No

_____

3. Would a dentist need capital resources to run an office?   Yes   No

_____

4. Are workers human resources?   Yes   No

_____

5. Are natural resources made from capital resources?   Yes   No

_____

6. Is a T-shirt factory involved in the production of a service? Yes   No

_____

Make Connections

Read each paragraph. Think about the meaning of the **bold** terms. Then, rewrite each paragraph using your own words. Do not use the vocabulary words in your sentences.

1. Supporters of women's **suffrage** worked for many years for an **amendment** to the **Constitution**. They finally succeeded in 1920.

   _____

   _____

   _____

2. In the **judicial** system, some cases are tried before a judge, and others go to a **jury**. Anyone accused of a crime is entitled to **representation** by a lawyer.

   _____

   _____

   _____

3. We read a news report that said the **legislative** branch of the state wants to raise taxes to protect **natural resources**. The **executive** branch wants to encourage **industry** by lowering rates of **taxation**.

   _____

   _____

   _____

 Challenge!

"No taxation without representation!" This is a well-known saying. It was first used by American colonists in the 1760s. What did they mean? Why did they say it? Research to find the answers.

_____

_____

_____

Make Connections

Read each pair of vocabulary words. Write the words where they fit in the sentences. Check the Student Dictionary for any meanings that you need.

1. production   industry
   Business managers in the automobile _____ are pleased to announce that _____ of cars is up.

2. labor   demand
   Hospitals are advertising jobs at high pay. The _____ for hospital workers is greater than the supply of _____.

3. census   Constitution
   Every ten years since 1790, a _____ has been taken of the population in all of the states, as required by the _____.

4. demand   supply
   The price of tomatoes is very low, so customers have high _____. But farmers don't like the low prices, so they produce fewer tomatoes. As a result, the _____ drops.

5. executive   legislative
   A governor leads the _____ branch of state government. A state's _____ branch has the power to pass laws.

6. supply   capital resources
   Drilling equipment and other _____ are needed to increase the _____ of oil and natural gas.

Word Alert!

The root *leg* comes from a Latin word for "law." Draw lines to match each word containing the root *leg* with its synonym containing *law*.

legal	lawmaker
illegal	laws
legislation	unlawful
legislator	lawful
legislative	lawmaking

Words Every Fourth Grader Needs to Know!

Play With Words

Code Words

Choose the word that fits in each sentence. Circle its letter.

1. Skilled labor is a ___.
   q branch of government
   r natural resource
   s human resource

2. Schools are supported by ___.
   u taxation
   v production
   w supply and demand

3. The ___ protects freedom of speech.
   e human resource
   f Bill of Rights
   g legislative branch

4. A ___ is like a head count.
   d jury
   e suffrage
   f census

5. Voters want ___ in Congress.
   q capital resources
   r representation
   s demand

6. ___ provides jobs.
   a Industry
   b The Bill of Rights
   c The Constitution

7. The U.S. President is in the ___ branch.
   e judicial
   f legislative
   g executive

8. The thirteenth ___ ended slavery.
   c jury
   d census
   e amendment

Write the circled letters in order. You will find the name for something that is necessary in a democracy.

_____

Play With Words

Two or Three

Read the clue. Find and circle the two or three words that match the clue.

1. Bill of Rights

   whfirstatentamendments

2. water, minerals, soil

   inaturalsalresourceswa

3. concerns of judges

   ysrijudicialghmattersti

4. U.S. Congress

   nfrlegislativeonbranchtof

5. forces that act on prices

   yousupplyyeandtydemandou

6. protection of voting rights

   casuffragennevamendmenter

7. when a census is taken

   seeveryeitenyearstyo

8. U.S. Constitution

   urnationalfulawture

Look back to find the letters you did NOT circle. Write them in order on the lines below to find a riddle and its answer.

___ ___ ___ ___   ___ ___   ___ ___ ___ ___ ___ ___

___ ___ ___ ___ ___   ___ ___

___ ___ ___ ___ ___   ___ ___   ___ ___ ___,   ___ ___ ___

___ ___ ___

___ ___ ___   ___ ___ ___ ___ ___   ___ ___ ___   ___ ___?

(___ ___ ___ ___   ___ ___ ___ ___ ___ ___ ___)

Name _____

Important Art Words You Need to Know!

Use this list to keep track of how well you know the new words.

0 = Don't Know   1 = Know It Somewhat   2 = Know It Well

___ ___ background
___ ___ brass
___ ___ collage
___ ___ conductor
___ ___ cue
___ ___ expression
___ ___ gesture
___ ___ improvise
___ ___ loom
___ ___ mosaic
___ ___ mural
___ ___ orchestra
___ ___ pastel
___ ___ percussion
___ ___ perspective
___ ___ portrait
___ ___ posture
___ ___ profile

___ ___ prop
___ ___ rhythmical
___ ___ script
___ ___ set
___ ___ shading
___ ___ stencil
___ ___ strings
___ ___ textile
___ ___ three-dimensional
___ ___ two-dimensional
___ ___ watercolor
___ ___ woodwinds

Explore a Word

Follow these steps.

1. Read the paragraph below. Think about the meaning of the **bold** word.

> Actors speak with **expression**. Musicians play with expression. A sculpture is an expression of the sculptor's idea. Art is an expression of feeling, experience, and more.

2. What do you think the word means? Write your idea.

   expression: _____

   _____

3. Write a sentence with the word **expression**. Show what it means.

   _____

   _____

4. Check the meaning of **expression** in the Student Dictionary.

5. If your sentence in step 3 matches the meaning, put a ✓ after it. If your sentence does not match the meaning, write a better sentence.

   _____

   _____

6. Make a simple drawing to show the meaning of **expression**.

Explore a Word

Read the sentences below. Think about the meaning of each **bold** word. Then, check the Student Dictionary.

> The hills in the painting are **rhythmical** curves in a repeating pattern.
>
> Jazz musicians start with a known song and then **improvise** as they play, creating something new.

Fill in the missing parts of the charts to show your understanding of the words *rhythmical* and *improvise*.

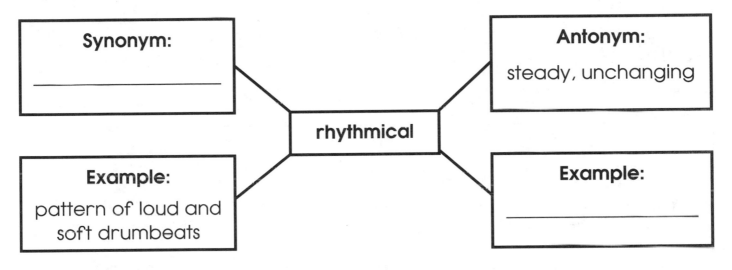

Synonym:
_____

Antonym:
steady, unchanging

rhythmical

Example:
pattern of loud and soft drumbeats

Example:
_____

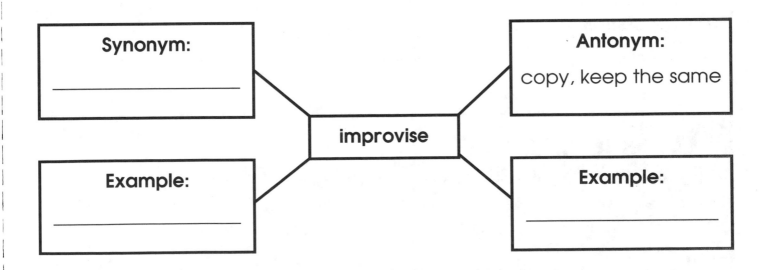

Synonym:
_____

Antonym:
copy, keep the same

improvise

Example:
_____

Example:
_____

Explore a Word

Read the sentences below. Think about the meaning of each **bold** word. Then, check the Student Dictionary.

> A weaver at a **loom** uses yarn or other fibers to create a **textile**. Knitted or woven textiles can be works of art.

Fill in the missing parts of the chart to show your understanding of each word.

	loom	textile
What Is It?		
What I Picture...		
How Do Artists Use It?		

📖 Look It Up!

Some words that look alike have different origins. These words have separately numbered entries in a dictionary. Look up the word *loom* in a classroom dictionary. Explain its two different meanings.

loom[1]: _____

loom[2]: _____

Words Every Fourth Grader Needs to Know!

Compare Words

Read the sentences below. Think about the meaning of each **bold** word. Then, check the Student Dictionary.

> The dancer stood in a stiff **posture**. As the music began, she slowly moved her arm in a welcoming **gesture**.

Complete each sentence with your own ideas about postures and gestures.

1. Sarah played the role of the queen in the play. Her posture was tall and straight. When she spoke to her servants, she made a gesture

    _____

    _____.

2. Matt played the role of a servant in the play. He made gestures of holding his palms together and bowing his head. His posture was

    _____

    _____.

3. The dancer's posture expressed a feeling of sadness. His gestures were _____

    _____.

4. The actor did not say a word. But his posture and gestures showed anger. For example, he _____

    _____.

 Look It Up!

Is the first part of *gesture* pronounced like *jest* or like *guest*? Use the pronunciation in the Student Dictionary to answer the question. Explain how you know you are right.

_____

_____

Compare Words

Read the paragraph below. Think about the meaning of each **bold** word. Then, check the Student Dictionary.

> Would you like to paint a **watercolor**? With thin paint called *watercolor*, you can show one color under another. You can make the colors flow and blur together. Work fast, because watercolor dries quickly. You might prefer to make a **pastel**. With chalk-like crayons called *pastels*, you can blend colors on the paper with your finger.

Circle the word that completes each sentence.

1. The artist used short, quick brushstrokes to show the leafy trees in this (watercolor/pastel).

2. The artist held the soft green chalk. Using it like a pencil, she made curved lines. In the finished (watercolor/pastel), the lines look like waves on water.

3. Artists sometimes choose (watercolor/pastel) because they want the paper to show through the paint.

4. The colors in a (watercolor/pastel) can rub off. Artists usually spray a glue-like material on the finished work to fix the colors in place.

5. The different strokes used in (watercolors/pastels) can make the artwork look like a painting.

6. When you view a (watercolor/pastel), look for the liquid, flowing qualities of the paint.

Words Every Fourth Grader Needs to Know!

Make Connections

Read the paragraph below. Think about the meaning of each **bold** term. Then, check the Student Dictionary.

> An artist draws a scene on a flat sheet of paper, which is **two-dimensional**. Yet the scene seems to have depth, length, and width. The scene looks **three-dimensional**. The artist has created **perspective** to show space and distance.

Underline the better ending to each sentence.

1. The house in Picture 1 is
   A. two-dimensional.
   B. three-dimensional.

2. Angled lines turn a flat house into a house that seems
   A. two-dimensional.
   B. three-dimensional.

3. Picture 2 shows a tree drawn smaller than the house because
   A. the artist is showing perspective.
   B. a two-dimensional tree is smaller than a house.

4. Picture 2 is made on
   A. two-dimensional paper.
   B. three-dimensional paper.

5. Artists use perspective to make
   A. three-dimensional shapes look flat.
   B. two-dimensional shapes look as if they have depth.

Make Connections

Read the paragraph below. Think about the meaning of each **bold** word. Then, check the Student Dictionary.

> The artist is drawing a **portrait** of a boy. She views the boy from the side, because this portrait is a **profile**. She adds **shading** to the boy's cheek, to show that it is round. She adds a **background** of a beach, even though she is painting indoors.

Complete each sentence with information about art. Use the vocabulary word in your answer.

I. profile
   If you look at the face on a dime, you will see _____

   _____.

2. background
   When you view a painting or a drawing, you see _____

   _____.

3. portrait
   A landscape shows an outdoor scene, but _____

   _____.

4. shading
   In real life, light and shadow fall differently on objects, so artists ____

   _____.

 Challenge!

On another sheet of paper, draw a picture to illustrate each of the vocabulary words on this page. Label each drawing with the vocabulary word.

Make Connections

Read the sentences below. Think about the meaning of each **bold** word. Then, check the Student Dictionary.

> Maria planned a **mosaic**. She arranged small colored tiles to make a design.
>
> Stefan cut out a **stencil** to print a repeating design.
>
> Cody made a **collage** of paper, feathers, and ribbon pasted to a sheet of cardboard.
>
> The whole class painted a **mural** on a concrete wall outside the school.

Underline the better ending to each sentence.

1. You often can see a mosaic on
   A. the floor of a public building.
   B. the roof of a tall building.

2. The place to see a mural is
   A. outdoors.
   B. on a wall.

3. A collage is interesting to look at because
   A. of the different materials used.
   B. of the unusual use of color.

4. When you make a print using a stencil, you
   A. cut a design into wood or another material.
   B. brush paint or ink through a hole.

5. Stencils are often used to
   A. decorate walls and wooden furniture.
   B. make a plan for a mural.

6. A mosaic collage is probably made of
   A. bits of paper glued to a larger paper.
   B. paper folded into three-dimensional shapes.

Make Connections

Read the paragraph below. Think about the meaning of each **bold** word. Then, check the Student Dictionary.

> Actors read a **script** to learn their lines. They note each **cue** that tells them when to enter or exit the stage. They learn when to sit or stand and how to handle each **prop** on the **set**.

Circle *Yes* or *No* for each question. Write your reason on the line.

1. Could a cue be something a character says? Yes No

   _____

2. Could a play have more than one set? Yes No

   _____

3. Is the set the same as the scenery? Yes No

   _____

4. If a character holds a flashlight, is the flashlight a cue? Yes No

   _____

5. Do actors use a script when performing? Yes No

   _____

6. Could a chair on a stage be a prop? Yes No

   _____

Word Alert!

The word *prop* is a shortened form of the longer word *property*, as in the term *theatrical property*. Use what you know about the words *theatrical* and *property* to explain the longer term.

_____

_____

Make Connections

Read the paragraph below. Think about the meaning of each **bold** word. Then, check the Student Dictionary.

> The musicians in an **orchestra** follow the signals of the **conductor**. The largest section of instruments is the **strings**. Violins, violas, cellos, and basses make up this section. The **woodwind** section usually includes flutes, oboes, clarinets, and bassoons. The **brass** section has trumpets, French horns, trombones, and tubas. Drums and cymbals are some of the instruments in the **percussion** section.

Label each picture with a vocabulary word.

1.

   _____

2.

   _____

3.

   _____

4.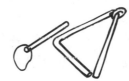

   _____

5.

   _____

6.

   _____

Use the words *conductor* and *orchestra* in a sentence to tell about a musical performance.

_____

_____

Make Connections

Read each list of vocabulary words. Cross out the word that does not fit with the others. Explain why this word does not belong. Check the Student Dictionary for any meanings that you need.

1. brass, loom, strings, woodwinds

   _____

2. percussion, perspective, shading, three-dimensional

   _____

3. textile, mosaic, collage, woodwind

   _____

4. stencil, gesture, expression, cue

   _____

5. orchestra, pastel, conductor, strings

   _____

6. rhythmical, mural, improvise, percussion

   _____

Play With Words

Code Words

Choose the word that fits in each sentence. Circle its letter.

1. Shaking a fist is a ___.
   a script
   b prop
   c gesture

2. Look for the tile pattern in a ___.
   q posture
   r mosaic
   s watercolor

3. Actors who forget their lines must ___.
   c set
   d script
   e improvise

4. An orchestra has ___.
   a strings
   b murals
   c textiles

5. A sculpture is ___.
   t three-dimensional
   u perspective
   v textile

6. A gesture is ___ of feeling.
   h a posture
   i an expression
   j a perspective

7. A person or an animal is in ___.
   t a stencil
   u a collage
   v a portrait

8. A knitted scarf is ___.
   d a pastel
   e a textile
   f a loom

Write the circled letters in order. You will find a word to describe the arts.

_____

Play With Words

Letter by Letter

Choose the word that fits with each clue. Write it letter by letter. Some letters will be inside circles.

background	improvise	script	woodwind	stencil
conductor	brass	rhythmical	shading	watercolor

1. To create without a plan __ __ __ __ __ Ⓞ __ __ __

2. A flute or an oboe __ __ __ __ __ Ⓞ __ __

3. A print from a cutout Ⓞ __ __ __ __ __ __

4. A leader with a baton __ __ __ __ Ⓞ __ __ __ __

5. A tuba or a trombone __ __ __ Ⓞ __

6. Having a beat __ __ __ __ __ __ __ __ __ Ⓞ

7. Use of darker line or color __ __ Ⓞ __ __ __ __

8. What looks distant __ __ __ __ Ⓞ __ __ __

9. A kind of painting __ __ Ⓞ __ __ __ __ __ __ __

10. A play in print __ __ Ⓞ __ __ __ __ __

Write the circled letters in order on the blanks. You will find the answer to this question. *What is the name for painting, drawing, sculpture, collage, and photography?*

__ __ __ __ __ __   __ __ __ __

Game Ideas and Suggestions

Use games and activities to help students better hear, see, and remember content-area vocabulary words. The suggestions on these pages can be used with the words in this book and with any other vocabulary words that students are learning.

Charades

Choose about ten vocabulary words. Write the words on slips of paper and display them. Give students time to think about the words before removing the slips. Then, divide the group into two teams. One team member chooses a slip, holds up fingers to indicate the number of syllables, and pantomimes the word. Teammates try to guess the word within a certain time limit.

Word Art

Help students select vocabulary words to depict as art. Encourage them to use letter shapes and arrangements to indicate what the words mean. Prompt students with questions, such as "How might you draw the letters of the word *three-dimensional*?" "Could you position the words *Arctic* and *Antarctic* to show their relationship?" Or "What might happen to the letters in *erosion*?"

Vocabulary Bingo

Reproduce and distribute the Vocabulary Bingo game card on page 119 for each student. Display a list of 40 vocabulary words, and have each student choose 25 words to write on his or her card. Write each of the 40 words on a separate slip of paper. Shuffle the slips, and choose one slip at a time. Instead of reading the word aloud, offer a clue about it. For example, for the word *insulator*, you might name the content area. "This is a science term having to do with energy." Or use a strong context sentence, with "blank" for the word. "The 'blank' is wrapped around the wire that conducts electricity." Students should check off the word if it is on their grids. The first student to complete four across, down, or diagonally calls out "Bingo" and reads aloud the four words.

Hink-Pinks

A *hink-pink* is a pair of rhyming words that answers a silly riddle. Use vocabulary words in the riddle, and have students, individually or in pairs, come up with the hink-pink reply. Encourage students to review their vocabulary lists and write their own hink-pink riddles for classmates. Examples of riddles:

* What do you call *judicial* candy? (judge fudge)
* What do you call a lovely *glacier*? (nice ice)
* What do you call a place for *magma*? (a hot spot)

Card Pairs

Use index cards cut in half to prepare a deck of 52 cards. Write 26 vocabulary words and 26 synonyms or short definitions on the cards. The cards can be used in a variety of games, such as Memory or Concentration. Here is one suggestion.

- **Go Fish!** for 2 to 5 Players
- Each player is dealt five cards. The remaining cards are placed face down in a pile.
- The player to the right of the dealer starts by setting aside any pairs. Then, he or she asks the player on the right for a card needed to make a pair. "Do you have *tundra*?" Or "Do you have the meaning of *tundra*?"
- If the holder has the requested card, he or she hands it over. If the holder does not have it, the player must "go fish" and draw the top card from the pile. If no match can be made, the next player takes a turn.
- The winner is the first player with no cards in hand or the player with the most pairs after all cards have been drawn.

Word Hunt

Emphasize that vocabulary words appear in print and online in a variety of informational resources. As you come across a vocabulary word—in a headline, news article, advertisement, or another resource—save the printed source or make a printout. Challenge students to read the text to find the vocabulary word and to explain what it means in the provided context.

Dictionary Guess

Have one student randomly choose a word from the Student Dictionary and read the definition aloud to the group. Partners or small groups then try to write the vocabulary word that matches the definition. Continue until each student has had a chance to choose a word and read its definition aloud. A point is awarded for each correct word.

Racetrack Games

Have students design their own racetrack board games or make one from a template you provide, such as the template on page 120. Here is one way to use the template.

- Select 25 vocabulary words for students to write in the spaces.
- Make a small cardboard spinner by drawing a circle divided into three sections labeled, 1, 2, and 3. The "spinner" can be a paper clip attached to a paper fastener.
- Provide small objects for students to use as markers.
- Each player spins, and the highest number goes first.
- A player spins and moves the marker the number of spaces shown. The player must say the word on the space and demonstrate knowledge of it by giving its definition or using it in a good context sentence.
- Players may use a dictionary to check the player's response. A player who is not correct loses a turn.
- The first player to reach the finish line wins.

Words Every Fourth Grader Needs to Know!

B	I	N	G	O

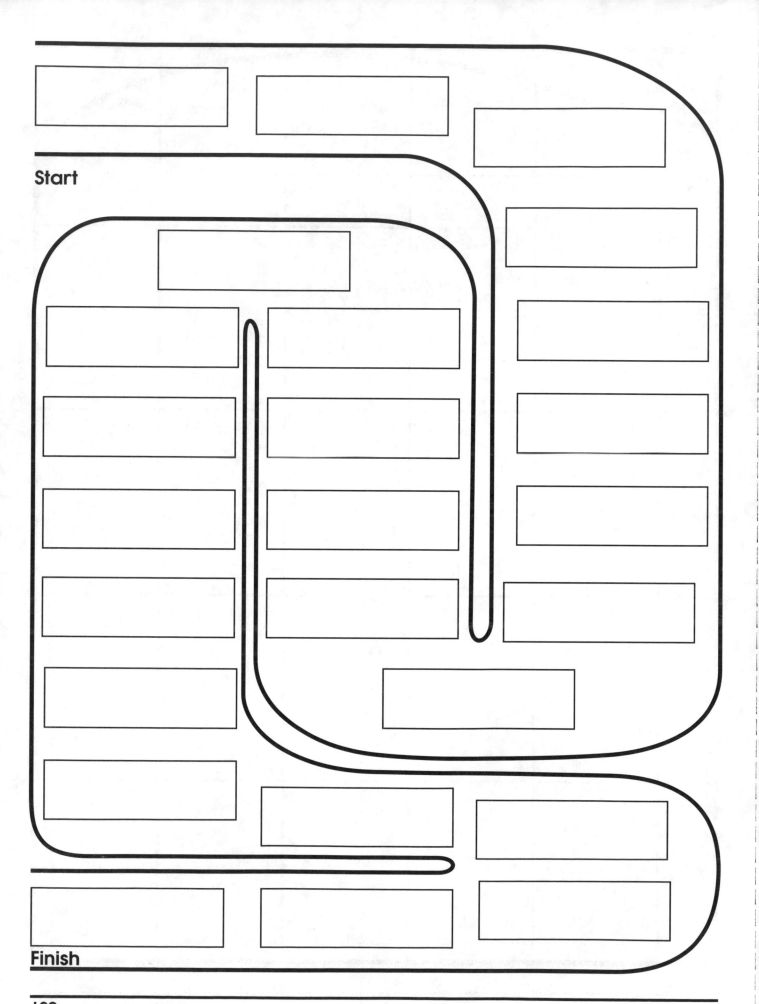

Start

Finish

Words Every Fourth Grader Needs to Know!

_____'s
Student Dictionary

Pronunciation Key

a	bat	oi	**oi**l
ā	day	o͞o	**too**
â	share	o͝o	took
ä	father	ou	**out**
e	net	u	**up**
ē	me	û	fur
i	big	th	**th**ink
ī	time	*th*	**th**at
o	hot	zh	treasure
ō	go	ə	**a**bout, happ**e**n,
ô	for		rob**i**n, lem**o**n,
			circ**u**s

Important Math Words I Need to Know!

centimeter (sen'tə mē'tər) *noun* A unit of length equal to $\frac{1}{100}$ of a meter and about $\frac{2}{5}$ of an inch.

circle graph (sûr'kəl graf) *noun* A diagram, also called a *pie chart*, that shows a circle divided into sections representing parts of a whole.

circumference (sûr kum'fər əns) *noun* The length of the boundary line of a circle.

common denominator (kom'ən di nom'ə nā'tər) *noun* A number that can be evenly divided by the denominators of two or more fractions. *The common denominator of the fractions $\frac{3}{4}$ and $\frac{3}{5}$ is 20.*

cubic unit (kyōō'bik yōō'nit) *noun* A measure of volume, or the space within a solid form, based on how many cubes will fit inside. *Cubic inches is an example of cubic units.*

cylinder (sil'in dər) *noun* A solid figure with two parallel circles at either base, or end. *A soup can is a cylinder.*

diameter (dī am'ə tər) *noun* A line segment between two points on a circle that passes through the center of the circle.

equation (i kwā'zhən) *noun* A number sentence with equal amounts on either side of the equal sign. *Example: 3 + 2 = 5*

equivalent fractions (i kwiv'ə lənt frak'shənz) *plural noun* Two or more fractions showing the same amount. $\frac{1}{2}$, $\frac{2}{4}$, *and* $\frac{50}{100}$ *are equivalent fractions.*

factor (fak'tər) *noun* A whole number that can divide another number without any remainder. *Factors of 12 include 1 and 12, 6 and 2, and 3 and 4.*

horizontal axis (hôr'ə zon'təl ak'sis) *noun* The line on a graph that goes from left to right, also called the *X-axis.*

inequality (in'i kwol'ə tē) *noun* A number sentence with different amounts on either side of the greater than (>) or the less than (<) sign. *Example: 3 + 2 > 4*

kilometer (kil'ə mē'tər or ki lom'ə tər) *noun* A unit of distance equal to 1,000 meters or about $\frac{5}{8}$ of a mile.

line graph (līn graf) *noun* A graph in which a line that rises, falls, or stays the same is used to show change over a period of time.

operation (op'ə rā'shən) *noun* A series of steps taken to get a result. *Addition and subtraction are examples of operations.*

percent (pər sent') *noun* Parts of one hundred; hundredths.

plane (plān) *noun* A flat surface that stretches in all directions without end. *A tabletop is part of a plane. adjective* Describing a flat surface. *A square is a plane figure.*

prism (priz'əm) *noun* A solid figure with two matching ends, or bases. Each base is a shape made of three or more lines. The faces of a prism are four-sided figures with opposite sides that are parallel.

probability (prob'ə bil'ə tē) *noun* The chance that an event will occur, stated as a fraction. *The probability that a tossed die will land on a particular side is $\frac{1}{6}$.*

pyramid (pir'ə mid) *noun* A solid figure

with a flat base of three or more sides and triangle faces that meet at a point at the top.

radius (rā'dē əs) *noun* A line segment from the center of a circle to any point on the circle.

rounding (round'ing) *noun* The act of raising or lowering a number to the nearest ten, hundred, thousand, and so on.

solid (sol'id) *noun* A shape that has length, width, and thickness. *A pyramid and a cone are both solids.* *adjective* Describing a shape that has length, width, and thickness. *A pyramid is a solid figure.*

vertical axis (vûr'ti kəl ak'sis) *noun* The line on a graph that goes up and down, also called the *Y-axis*.

volume (vol'yōōm) *noun* The measure of the space inside a solid figure.

More Math Words I Need to Know:

_____

_____

_____

_____

_____

_____

_____

_____

_____

_____

_____

_____

_____

Important Science and Health Words I Need to Know!

artery (är'tə rē) *noun* One of the blood vessels that carries blood from the heart to all the parts of the body.

cell (sel) *noun* The basic unit of living matter, too tiny to see.

circuit (sûr'kit) *noun* The path of an electric current.

conductor (kən duk'tər) *noun* A material that allows energy to pass through it. *Metals, such as gold and silver, are good conductors.*

crust (krust) *noun* The solid outer layer of the Earth.

digestion (di jes'chən or dī jes'chən) *noun* The process by which food is changed into forms that can be used by the body.

electric current (i lek'trik kûr'ənt) *noun* The movement or flow of positive or negative electric charges.

erupt (i rupt') *verb* To burst forth powerfully. *Some volcanoes erupt frequently.*

erosion (i rō'zhən) *noun* The process by which rock and soil are moved from one location to another.

esophagus (i sof'ə gəs) *noun* The tube that carries food from the mouth to the stomach.

fault (fôlt) *noun* A break in the Earth's crust, in which rocks on opposite sides slide past each other.

fossil (fos'əl) *noun* The signs or preserved remains of a living thing from thousands or millions of years ago. *The fossils of shells found in rocks show that the land was once under water.*

frequency (frē'kwən sē) *noun* The number of sound waves that pass a particular point each second.

igneous (ig'nē əs] *adjective* Formed from molten rock that has cooled and hardened. *Some igneous rocks form from lava.*

insulator (in'sə lā'tər) *noun* A material that slows or prevents the passage of energy from another material. *Rubber is a good electric insulator.*

intensity (in ten'si tē) *noun* The measure of the power of particular sound waves. *Sound waves with high intensity are loud.*

large intestine (lärj in tes'tin) *noun* The lower of the two tubes below the stomach. Food materials that the body cannot use enter the large intestine, which has the main job of preparing waste to leave the body.

lava (lä'və) *noun* A form of molten rock that flows from a volcano.

magma (mag'mə) *noun* Rock heated to extremely high temperatures below the Earth's crust. Magma is molten, or melted by heat.

mantle (man'tl) *noun* The layers of the Earth that lie between the crust and the inner regions that form the core.

metamorphic (met'ə môr'fik) *adjective* Formed from rock that has been changed by heat and pressure within the Earth. *Marble is a metamorphic rock.*

nucleus (noo'klē əs) *noun* The control

center of a living cell, which directs the cell's activities.

organ (ôr'gən) *noun* A part of a living thing that performs a function. *The lungs are organs that we use for breathing.*

pitch (pich) *noun* The level of how high or low a sound seems to us. The pitch of a sound depends on how quickly the sound waves are vibrating.

rock cycle (rok sī'kəl) *noun* A series of stages in which one type of rock changes into another. The rock cycle is a way of explaining how rocks change over time.

sedimentary (sed'ə men'tə rē) *adjective* Formed from rock made of layers of material that have hardened. *Limestone is a sedimentary rock.*

small intestine (smôl in tes'tin) *noun* The long tube directly below the stomach. The small intestine prepares nutrients to enter the blood vessels and feed the body.

stomach (stum'ək) *noun* The organ of digestion between the esophagus and the small intestine, where food begins to be broken down into nutrients that feed the body.

tissue (tish'yōō) *noun* Groupings of similar cells that share a function in the body. *Nerve tissue is one kind of tissue.*

vein (vān) *noun* One of the blood vessels that carry blood from all parts of the body to the heart.

vibrate (vī'brāt') *verb* To move back and forth very quickly.

volcano (vol kā'nō) *noun* An opening in the Earth's crust through which molten rock, cinders, ash, and gases flow or burst out.

volume (vol'yōōm) *noun* The loudness of a sound.

wavelength (wāv length) *noun* The distance between a point on one wave and a point in the same position on the next wave.

weathering (we*th*'ər ing) *noun* The action of wind, rain, ice, heat, and other forces on rocks. Weathering breaks rocks apart.

More Science and Health Words I Need to Know:

_____

_____

_____

_____

_____

Important Technology Words I Need to Know!

durable (dûr'ə bəl) *adjective* Able to withstand hard use.

effort (ef'ərt) *noun* The force applied to a simple machine. *It takes less effort to push a weight up a ramp than to lift it with muscle power.*

electronic (i lek'tron'ik) *adjective* Having to do with electric signals made by controlling the flow and direction of electric charges. *Communication over cell phones and the Internet depends on electronic systems.*

friction (frik'shən) *noun* A force that works against or slows down an object's motion. *Objects slide on ice because an icy surface has less friction than a bumpy surface.*

fulcrum (fool'krəm) *noun* The point on which a lever pivots, or turns.

function (funk'shən) *noun* The purpose or use of something. *Each part of a machine has a function.* *verb* To serve a purpose.

gravity (grav'i tē) *noun* The force of attraction between objects, such as the Earth and the Sun, and between the Earth and objects on the Earth's surface. *The weight of an object depends on the force of gravity that acts on it.*

icon (ī'kon') *noun* A small picture on a computer screen that represents a program or task. *Click on the icon of a camera to open a photography program.*

innovation (in'ə vā'shən) *noun* An improvement or change to something; a new way of doing something; an invention. *Reducing the use of gasoline depends on innovations to automobiles.*

lever (lē'vər or lev'ər) *noun* A simple machine made of a bar that turns on a support and is used to lift loads. *A wheelbarrow is one type of lever.*

load (lōd) *noun* The weight, or force, of an object that is lifted by a simple machine.

mechanical (mi kan'i kəl) *adjective* Having to do with machines.

memory (mem'ə rē) *noun* The data and instructions stored on a computer chip. *Random access memory, or RAM, enables the user of a personal computer to work with programs.*

menu (men'yoo) *noun* A list of options, or choices, displayed on a computer screen.

multimedia (mul'tē mē' dē ə) *noun* A computer program that combines sound, text, photos, video, and graphics.

nonrenewable (non'ri noo'ə bəl) *adjective* Having to do with an energy source or a natural resource that cannot be replaced after it is used.

processor (pros'es'ər or prō'ses'ər) *noun* The part of a computer that controls, or processes, electronic information.

reliable (ri lī'ə bəl) *adjective* Giving the same results each time. *A reliable machine performs the same actions each time it is used.*

renewable (ri noo'ə bəl) *adjective* Having to do with an energy source or a natural resource that does not run out or that can grow again.

structure (struk'chər) *noun* The arrangement of parts. *The structure of a leaf includes a stem.*

More Technology Words I Need to Know:

_____

_____

_____

_____

_____

_____

_____

_____

_____

_____

_____

_____

_____

_____

_____

_____

_____

_____

_____

Important Language Arts Words I Need to Know!

adjective (aj'ik tiv) *noun* A word that describes a noun or a pronoun. *One cloud is dark and heavy.*

adverb (ad'vûrb) *noun* A word that describes a verb, an adjective, or another adverb. *He spoke very loudly.*

agreement (əgrē'mənt) *noun* A grammar rule that says the verb must match the number of subjects. *Correct: That boy eats fast. Incorrect: That boy eat fast.*

apostrophe (ə pos'trə fē) *noun* A mark that replaces missing letters in a contraction (*don't*), shows ownership (*David's*), or shows the plural of numbers and letters (*three X's*).

compare and contrast (kəm pâr' and kən trast') *verb* To describe things that are alike and things that are different.

conjunction (kən jungk'shən) *noun* A word that joins words or parts of a sentence. *And*, *but*, and *or* are conjunctions.

essay (es'ā) *noun* A short written work on a topic. An essay usually tells about the writer's experiences and viewpoint.

folktale (fōk'tāl') *noun* A story from long ago that was told orally before it was written down.

idiom (id'ē əm) *noun* A group of words or a saying that has a special meaning. *The idiom* on top of the world *means "feeling happy."*

irregular plural (i reg'yə lər plûr'əl) *noun* The form of a noun that names more than one but is not made by adding *s* or *es*. *Correct: many women; Incorrect: many womans*

metaphor (met'ə fôr') *noun* A kind of comparison in which one thing is said to be another. *Example: The moon is a silver coin.*

mystery (mis'tə rē) *noun* A kind of story that usually involves a crime or puzzle that needs to be solved.

narrator (nar'āt ər) *noun* A storyteller. A narrator can be a character in a story who uses pronouns such as *I* and *me* to tell what happens. A narrator can also be an unknown character outside the story who uses *he*, *she*, and *they* to tell what happens.

outline (out'līn') *noun* A list of ideas and information to include in a written work. *verb* To make a planning list for a written work.

persuade (pûr swād') *verb* To try to get others to agree with your viewpoint or do what you ask.

plot (plot) *noun* The action in a story. A plot often begins with a problem, continues with attempts to solve the problem, reaches a high point where the problem is or is not solved, and then drops to a conclusion.

possession (pə zesh'ən) *noun* Ownership. Nouns and pronouns can show possession, or who owns or has something. *Examples: the boy's dog, the dogs' collars, their house*

prefix (prē'fiks) *noun* A word part added before a word to change its meaning or change how it is used in a sentence. *Examples: misbehave, unbutton, replay*

pronoun (prō'noun') *noun* A word that takes the place of a noun. The words *I, he, you, her, it,* and *them* are examples

Words Every Fourth Grader Needs to Know!

of pronouns.

punctuation (pungk'chŏŏ ā'shən) *noun* The marks used to signal pauses and other information in a sentence. Marks of punctuation include commas, periods, and semicolons.

research (ri sûrch' or rē'sûrch') *noun* Asking questions and looking for information that will provide answers.

simile (sim'ə lē) *noun* A kind of comparison, using *like* or *as*, that points out a similarity in things that are not usually thought of as alike. *Example: a stare as cold as an icicle*

subject (sub'jekt') *noun* The part of a sentence that tells who or what. *The girls talked. That phone is small. Time went by.*

suffix (suf'iks) *noun* A word part added to the end of a word to change its meaning or change how it is used in a sentence. *Examples: happiness, careful, slowly*

summarize (sum'ə rīz) *verb* To tell only the most important parts of a story or the main ideas in an informational work; to sum up

suspense (sə spens') *noun* Waiting with nervousness and excitement for the next events in a story.

thesaurus (thə sôr'əs) *noun* A book of synonyms, or words with similar meanings. A thesaurus may also include antonyms, or words with opposite meanings.

topic sentence (top'ik sen'təns) *noun* A sentence that states the main idea of a paragraph or section. A topic sentence is often the first sentence of a paragraph.

trickster (trik'stər) *noun* A selfish and mischief-making character who often appears in folktales and legends.

word origin (wûrd ôr'ə jin) *noun* The history of a word, showing how it changed over time as it was used by speakers of different languages.

More Language Arts Words I Need to Know:

_____

_____

_____

_____

_____

_____

_____

Important History Words I Need to Know!

agriculture (ag'ri kul'chər) *noun* The management of soil and raising of crops and livestock; farming.

ally (al'ī) *noun* A person, group, or nation that has joined with another for a shared purpose. *verb* (ə lī') To work together or to fight a shared enemy.

ancestor (an'ses'tər) *noun* A grandparent's parent or earlier person from whom one is descended.

conflict (kon'flikt) *noun* **1.** A dispute or lasting fight. **2.** A struggle between opposite feelings or beliefs. *verb* (kən flikt') To differ or disagree. *Our opinions conflict, but we can still be friends.*

debate (di bāt') *noun* A discussion in which opposing sides express their views. *verb* To give reasons for and against a plan or an opinion.

equality (i kwol'i tē) *noun* The state of being equal and having the same rights as others.

folklore (fōk'lôr') *noun* The songs, stories, and beliefs of a people that are passed down through time.

found (found) *verb* To set up for the first time. *Spain wanted to found settlements in Florida.*

frontier (frun tēr') *noun* The edge of a settled area of land, beyond which is wilderness.

game (gām) *noun* Wild animals or birds that are hunted for food or sport.

generation (jen'ə ra'shən) *noun* **1.** All of the family members at the same level of descent from an ancestor. *Parents and children are two generations.* **2.** A period of about 30 years, the time between the birth of parents and their children.

hardship (härd'ship) *noun* A problem or difficulty that causes suffering.

heritage (her'i tij) *noun* Ideas and things passed down over time. *Americans' musical heritage includes jazz and rock music.*

hunter-gatherers (hun'tər ga*th*'ər ərz) *plural noun* People who find wild sources of food, either by killing animals or by collecting plants, roots, and fruits.

independence (in'di pen'dəns) *noun* Having self-government; not being ruled by another nation. *African colonies fought for independence from European rulers.*

inhabitant (in hab'i tənt) *noun* Someone who lives in a particular place. *The inhabitants of the island reach the mainland by boat.*

integration (in'ti grā'shən) *noun* The act of making a school, park, bus, or other public place open to people of all races.

international (in'tər nash'ə nəl) *adjective* Involving two or more countries. *Ten nations signed the international trade agreement.*

irrigation (ir'i gā'shən) *noun* The watering of crops using constructions, such as ditches and pipes.

Loyalist (loi'ə list) *noun* An American colonist who wanted the colonies to remain under British rule.

migration (mī grā'shən) *noun* The movement of people or animals from one place to another.

militia (m lish') *noun* A group of citizens with special training to fight as soldiers when called upon.

national (nash'ə nəl) *adjective* Having to do with a country or nation. *Every country has its own national flag.*

nomadic (nō mad'ik) *adjective* Moving from place to place in search of food; roaming.

patriot (pā'trē ət) *noun* A person who loves and defends his or her country.

Patriot (pā'trē ət) *noun* An American colonist who wanted the colonies to be free of British rule. *Patriots fought against British troops.*

pioneer (pī'ə nēr') *noun* The first settler in a region.

primary source (prī'mer ē sôrs) *noun* A diary, account, speech, photograph, letter, document, or other material that gives information about a historical event from the viewpoint of people who were involved in it.

protest (prō'test) *noun* An objection to something. *Example: a protest against high taxes. verb* (prə test') To complain about or object to. *Voters signed a document to protest higher taxes.*

ritual (rich'oo əl) *noun* A ceremony performed in a certain way. *The crowning of a new king was a ritual that lasted days.*

secondary source (sek'ən der'ē sôrs) *noun* A report, article, painting, or other material that gives information about a historical event based on research of that event.

segregation (seg'ri gā'shən) *noun* The act of setting one group apart from the main group, often based on race or gender.

statehood (stāt'hood') *noun* The condition of being a full member of the Union, a state in the United States.

territory (ter'i tôr'ē) *noun* **1.** An area of land. **2.** A region that belongs to the United States but is not a state.

tradition (trə dish'ən) *noun* A belief or custom that is passed down from each generation to the next.

treaty (trē'tē) *noun* A formal agreement between nations.

More History Words I Need to Know:

_____

_____

_____

_____

_____

_____

Important Geography Words I Need to Know!

adapt (ə dapt') *verb* To change one's body, behavior, or way of life in order to live in a changed environment.

Antarctic (ant ärk'tik) *noun, adjective* The region that includes the southernmost ocean, the South Pole, and the continent of Antarctica.

Arctic (ärk'tik) *noun, adjective* The region that includes the northernmost ocean, the North Pole, and the northern parts of North America, Asia, and Europe.

biome (bī'ōm) *noun* A large area that has a distinct community of plants and animals. *Plants that have adapted to little rainfall are part of a desert biome.*

canyon (kan'yən) *noun* A narrow and deep opening in the Earth, carved by a river or other running water. *At the bottom of the canyon, we looked up at the steep walls of rock on either side.*

compass rose (kum'pəs rōz) *noun* The circular symbol on a map that shows directions, like the points of a compass.

conservation (kon'sûr vā'shən) *noun* The protection and management of natural resources, natural environments, and wildlife.

delta (del'tə) *noun* The land, often in the shape of a triangle, that forms at the mouth of a river. The river carries soil that builds up to form a delta.

drought (drout) *noun* A long period without the rain that usually falls during that time.

equator (i kwā'tər) *noun* The imaginary circle that runs east-west to divide the globe into a northern half and a southern half.

floodplain (flud'plān') *noun* The flat land on either side of a river, which floods when the river overflows.

glacier (glā'shər) *noun* A great mass of ice formed from snow that has fallen over many years. A glacier moves slowly over land.

hemisphere (hem'i sfēr') *noun* Half of the globe. The globe has an eastern and a western hemisphere. It also has a northern and a southern hemisphere.

latitude (lat'i tōōd') *noun* The distance on the Earth's surface north or south of the equator, measured in degrees. Lines of latitude run east-west around the globe.

longitude (lonj'i tōōd') *noun* The distance on the Earth's surface east or west of an imaginary line called the *prime meridian*, measured in degrees. Lines of longitude run north-south between the Poles.

physical feature (fiz'i kəl fē'chər) *noun* A landform or a body of water.

plateau (pla'tō) *noun* A large area of high and fairly flat land.

population (pop'yə lā'shən) *noun* All of the people living in a region.

region (rē'jən) *noun* **1.** An area of the Earth's surface with shared characteristics. Climate, landforms, or plant life are some of the characteristics of a region. **2.** Any area in which people share cultural elements, such as language, religion, or practices.

strait (strāt) *noun* A narrow body of water that connects two larger bodies of water.

swamp (swomp) *noun* A low-lying land

with trees, shrubs, and woody plants that are adapted to flooding. Swamps often develop near rivers and streams.

tropics (trop'iks) *noun* The region of the Earth's surface between the two lines of latitude known as the Tropic of Cancer, which is north of the equator, and the Tropic of Capricorn, which is south of the equator.

tundra (tun'drə) *noun* The Arctic area between the treeline and the polar ice. The tundra has only low-lying plants, and the soil below the surface is permanently frozen.

vegetation (vej'i tā'shən) *noun* Plant life.

wetland (wet'land') *noun* A low-lying land that is flooded for all or part of the year. *Swamps, marshes, and bogs are examples of wetlands.*

More Geography Words I Need to Know:

_____

_____

_____

_____

_____

_____

_____

_____

_____

_____

_____

Important Civics and Economics Words I Need to Know!

amendment (ə mend'ment) *noun* A change or an addition to a law, a bill, or a constitution.

Bill of Rights ('bil uv 'rīts) *noun* The first ten amendments to the U.S. Constitution, which protect basic human rights, such as freedom of speech and the right to a fair trial.

branches of government (branch'iz uv guv'ûrn ment) *noun* The three main groups that share power in the United States, as well as in other countries and states. The three groups are the lawmakers (legislative branch), the leaders who carry out the laws (executive branch), and the judges who make decisions about laws (judicial branch).

capital resources (kap'i təl rē'sôrs əz) *noun* Goods produced and used to make other goods and services. Capital resources can be re-used and include tools, machines, and equipment.

census (sen'səs) *noun* A count of the population, performed by a government agency. A census includes information about who is in a country, and where and how they live.

Constitution (kon'sti tōo' shən) *noun* The basic law of the United States. The Constitution lays out the system of government for the nation.

demand (di mand') *noun* The measure of buyers' desire for and willingness to pay for a product or service at different prices. *When the price of strawberries is high, the demand for them is usually low.*

executive (ig zek'yə tiv) *adjective* Of the branch of government that carries out the law. *The U.S. Secretary of Agriculture is a member of the executive branch.*

human resources (hyōo'mən rē'sôrs əz) *noun* The people who do the varied work involved in producing goods and services.

industry (in'də strē) *noun* **1.** The combination of business activities involved in making a product. **2.** The businesses involved in making goods or providing services in a broad category, such as manufacturing automobiles or selling real estate.

judicial (jōo'dish'əl) *adjective* Having to do with judges and judgments in courts of law.

jury (jōor'ē) *noun* A group of people selected to listen to both sides of a legal case and reach a decision, called a *verdict.*

labor (lā'bər) *noun* The workers in a job or industry.

legislative (lej'i slā'tiv) *adjective* Of the branch of government that makes the laws.

natural resources (nach'ər əl rē'sôrs əz) *noun* Sources provided by nature and used by people to make products. *Timber, iron ore, and water are natural resources.*

production (prə duk'shən) *noun* **1.** The making of goods and services. **2.** The goods or services produced by a business.

representation (rep'ri zen tā'shən) *noun*

The right to have lawmakers serve as the agents of citizens and express the citizens' views.

suffrage (suf'rij) *noun* The right to vote.

supply (sə plī') *noun* The amount of a product or a service that is available for sale at different prices. *When the supply of strawberries is low, the price tends to be high.*

taxation (tak sā'shən) *noun* The plan and rules by which payments to the government are made; the act of setting taxes.

More Civics and Economics Words I Need to Know:

_____

_____

_____

_____

_____

_____

_____

_____

_____

_____

_____

_____

_____

_____

_____

Important Art Words I Need to Know!

background (bak'ground') *noun* In a painting or other artwork, the scene or part that is behind the other parts.

brass (bras) *noun, adjective* The section of a band or an orchestra that has brass instruments. Brass instruments, such as the trumpet and French horn, are made of brass or another metal and played by blowing air into a mouthpiece.

collage (kə läzh') *noun* A form of artwork in which bits of paper or other objects are pasted to a paper or other flat surface.

conductor (kən duk'tər) *noun* The leader of an orchestra or a chorus. The conductor uses a baton to signal musicians or singers and to show the rate of speed at which the music should be played.

cue (kyoo) *noun* In a play or performance, the words or action that signals an actor or a performer to say or do something.

expression (ik spresh'ən) *noun* The communication of ideas or feelings through artwork, music, dance, acting, and other forms of art.

gesture (jes'chər) *noun* A movement of the hands, arms, legs, feet, head, or body to show an idea or a feeling. *A snap of the fingers is a gesture that means "I've got it!"* *verb* To make a movement of a body part to show an idea or a feeling.

improvise (im'prə vīz) *verb* To perform music or to act in a play without a prepared plan.

loom (loom) *noun* A frame that holds yarn or thread that is being woven into cloth.

mosaic (mō zā'ik) *noun* A picture or design made with small colored pieces of glass, stone, tile, or other materials.

mural (myoo'rəl) *noun* A large picture painted directly on a wall.

orchestra (ôr'ki strə) *noun* A large group of musicians who play together on various instruments and are led by a conductor. *Most of the instruments in a symphony orchestra are strings.*

pastel (pas tel') *noun* **1.** A chalk-like crayon. **2.** A picture made with pastel crayons.

percussion (pûr kush'ən) *noun, adjective* The section of a band or an orchestra made of instruments that are struck, shaken, or scraped. *Drums, xylophones, and maracas are percussion instruments.*

perspective (pûr spek'tiv) *noun* An artist's use of line and space in ways that suggest real-life distances. Changing the size of figures in a drawing is one way to show perspective. For example, smaller figures seem farther away.

portrait (pôr'trit) *noun* A drawing, painting, or photograph of a real person, especially of the face.

posture (pos'chər) *noun* A way of holding the body while standing or sitting. *Standing with your shoulders back is a proud posture.*

profile (prō'fīl') *noun* A person's head as seen from the side.

prop (prop) *noun* Any object on a stage that is not part of the scenery or costumes. Tables and chairs are props in the set. Actors also hold and use props, such as a glass or a telephone.

rhythmical (ri*th*'mik əl) *adjective* Having a pattern that repeats in a regular way. Musical beats are rhythmical. Patterns of lines, shapes, and colors can be rhythmical. Movements and speech can be rhythmical, too.

script (skript) *noun* The printed form of a play, movie, or broadcast. A script includes the words to be spoken, descriptions of the setting, and directions to the performers.

set (set) *noun* The scenery, furniture, and other objects that are on a stage for each scene of a play or performance.

shading (shā'ding) *noun* The use of lines and marks to fill in areas of a drawing or a painting to suggest a change from light to dark.

stencil (sten'sil) *noun* A paper or other flat material with sections that are cut out. Ink or paint is pressed through the cutout onto the printing surface.

strings (stringz) *noun* The section of an orchestra made of stringed instruments. *Violins and cellos are examples of strings.*

textile (teks'tīl) *noun* A cloth made by weaving or knitting.

three-dimensional (thrē'di men'shə nəl) *adjective* Having length, width, and depth. Also called *3-D.*

two-dimensional (too'di men'shə nəl) *adjective* Having length and width; flat.

watercolor (wô'tûr kul'ər) *noun* **1.** A paint that is easy to see through, made with powdered colors and water. **2.** A painting made with watercolors.

woodwinds (wood winz) *noun* The section of an orchestra made of wind instruments. Woodwinds, such as clarinets and oboes, have reeds in the mouthpiece. The flute is a woodwind in which air passes over the mouthpiece.

More Art Words I Need to Know:

_____

_____

_____

_____

_____

_____

_____

_____

Notes

Answer Key

Math

Page 6
Students use this page to assess their own knowledge of *probability*. Encourage students to explain how their drawing helps them remember word meaning.

Page 7
Sample responses: (for 5 km) a road race that takes about 15–20 minutes; (for 10 cm) crayon length; (for 10 km) farthest distance I've ridden a bike; (for school-home distance) 3 km; (for length of pencil) 19 cm
Word Alert! 1. 1/100 of a liter, or about 1 tablespoon or a few drops; 2. 1,000 liters, or about 4,000 cups

Page 8
1. plane; 2. plane; 3. solid; 4. solid; 5. plane; 6. solid
Look It Up! Definitions will vary.

Page 9
Sample responses for chart:
Both: number sentences; have two sides; show how amounts are related
Equation: both sides the same; uses equals sign; can switch left and right numbers without changing meaning
Inequality: each side different; two possible signs; cannot switch the numbers unless you change the sign
Word Alert! Sample response: All the words have to do with two things that are in or not in balance

Page 10
Sample responses:
(1) Subtracting, multiplying, and estimating are common operations.
(2) Use rounding when you don't need to know the exact amount.
(3) The number in the ones place, 7, is more than 5, so round up. The 2 in the tens place becomes 3. The rounded number is 630.
(4) The number 2 in the tens place is less than 5, so round down. The number in the hundreds place stays the same. The rounded number is 600.

Page 11
Students' reasons will vary.
1. No, the diameter is twice the length of the radius.
2. Yes, one end of a radius touches the center of a circle.
3. No, the circumference is curved.
4. Yes, a diameter crosses a circle through the center.
5. No, the radius must touch the center.
6. No, a square has a perimeter.

Page 12
1. Students' drawings should show a circle with one half labeled $\frac{1}{2}$ and the other labeled $\frac{2}{4}, \frac{3}{6}, \frac{4}{8}$ or another equivalent fraction.
2. Students' drawings should show a square divided into four equal sections, with one shaded section and three striped sections.
3. Sample response: $\frac{1}{2} + \frac{1}{4} = \frac{2}{4} + \frac{1}{4} = \frac{3}{4}$
4. Sample responses: $4 \times 1 = 4$; $1 \times 253 = 253$
Challenge! Sample response:
$$\frac{9}{12} \div \frac{3}{3} = \frac{3}{4}$$
$$\frac{75}{100} \div \frac{25}{25} = \frac{3}{4}$$

Page 13
1. triangle; 2. four; 3. circle; 4. volume; 5. Sample response: bathtub
Second activity: Students' drawing captions will vary. Sample: This giant cube has a volume of 27 cubic units.

Page 14
Sample caption for completed circle graph: This circle graph shows that soccer is much more popular than skateboarding.
Sample caption for completed line graph: This line graph shows that I read the most pages on Monday and the fewest pages on Saturday.

Page 15
1. percent, probability; 2. cylinder, volume; 3. equation, operation; 4. circle graph, inequality; 5. plane, centimeter; 6. diameter, rounding
Second activity: Students' sentences will vary.

Page 16
The letters spell *estimate*.

Page 17
1. pyramid; 2. rounding; 3. cubic; 4. radius; 5. kilometer; 6. cylinder; 7. prism; 8. inequality; Answer to message: You did it!

Page 18
1. circle graph; 2. equivalent fractions; 3. common denominator; 4. line graph; 5. horizontal axis; 6. vertical axis
Caption Match: Students' drawings should show a circle with a diameter of about 4 cm (between 1 1/2 and 2 inches) with 20 percent shading to suggest a sphere and additional details.

Science and Health

Page 20
Students use this page to assess their own knowledge of *fossil*. Encourage students to explain how their drawing helps them remember word meaning.

Page 21
1. erosion; 2. weathering; 3. erosion; 4. weathering; 5. erosion
Students' captions should show that weathering changes the mountain's appearance and erosion takes rocks and soil away.

Page 22
1. arteries; 2. veins; 3. arteries; 4. veins; 5. artery
Students' diagrams should show arteries going away from the heart and veins going toward it.

Page 23
Sample response: First, attach the wire to the battery. Make sure that you connect the wire, not the plastic insulator. Then, put the switch down to complete the circuit. Electric current will flow through the wire conductor.
Look It Up! Students' drawings should show a conductor of music, a train conductor, and a conductor of electricity.

Answer Key

Page 24
Students' drawings should show a curved surface representing the Earth, with a thin outer layer of crust, the thick section of mantle under it, and an outer and inner core. Sample caption: A fault can form between the plates made of the crust and the top part of the mantle.
Look It Up! Numbers and meanings will vary.

Page 25
Sample response: When this volcano erupts, lava is flowing from the top. The magma is rising from the mantle below.
Word Alert! Sample responses: **1.** to break out; **2.** to make something break up, like when you disrupt a meeting; **3.** to break into something, like when you interrupt a conversation; **4.** to break, like a rupture in the appendix or another body part

Page 26
1. A; **2.** A; **3.** B; **4.** A

Page 27
Students' reasons will vary.
1. No, the cells of muscle tissue are different from the cells of bone.
2. Yes, the stomach is an organ of digestion.
3. No, tissues make up organs, not the other way around.
4. Yes, a nucleus is the central part of a cell.
1. nucleus; **2.** cell; **3.** organ; **4.** tissue

Page 28
1. digestion; **2.** esophagus; **3.** esophagus; **4.** stomach; **5.** small intestine; **6.** small intestine; **7.** large intestine; **8.** digestion

Page 29
Sample responses:
1. ...I couldn't hit it hard enough to give the sound the intensity I wanted. It was not loud enough.
2. ...make the sound waves in the air vibrate faster, at a higher frequency.
3. ...glass vibrates, sending sound waves through the air.
4. ...didn't want to disturb the neighbors with a high volume of sound.
5. ...a low pitch. His voice is much deeper than ours.
6. ...have ears that detect wavelengths that are shorter or longer than the ones we can hear.

Page 30
1. sedimentary rocks, fossils; **2.** weathering, erosion; **3.** organ, digestion; **4.** Arteries, Veins; **5.** conductor, insulator; **6.** vibrate, pitch
Second activity: Students' sentences will vary.

Page 31
Students' reasons will vary.
1. Cross out *nucleus*; it's part of a cell and doesn't have to do with rocks.
2. Cross out *circuit*; it has to do with electric current, not rocks.
3. Cross out *crust*; it has to do with the Earth, not the body.
4. Cross out *erupt*; it's not a kind of rock.
5. Cross out *fault*; it doesn't have to do with sound waves.
6. Cross out *mantle*; it's inside the Earth, not inside the body.

Page 32
The letters spell *volcanic*.

Page 33
1. lava; **2.** crust; **3.** stomach; **4.** intestine; **5.** digestion; **6.** circuit; **7.** nucleus; **8.** vibrate; **9.** igneous; **10.** erosion.
Answer to riddle: Both need a conductor.

Page 34
Answers spell *experiment*.

Technology

Page 36
Students use this page to assess their own knowledge of *innovation*. Encourage students to explain how their drawing helps them remember word meaning.

Page 37
Sample responses for web:
Name: Multimedia means "many ways of giving information or communicating."
Examples: video game, multimedia encyclopedia, a presentation on a screen using software
Descriptive words: flashy, lively, attention-grabbing, interesting
Purposes: to entertain, to give information

Page 38
Students' drawings should show any common product, such as a pair of scissors or a car. Sample captions: My dad's car is reliable because it always starts when he turns the key. It has 150,000 miles on it, so it must be durable.
Word Alert! Sample responses: **1.** can be depended on to work right; **2.** lasts a long time without breaking down.

Page 39
Sample responses:
1. ...holding up to forces. A bridge holds up a roadway, and a skeleton holds up the body.
2. ...allows air to flow over the wing and under it so that there is lift. Lift keeps the bird and the plane up in the air.
3. ...pushing liquids to all parts of the body without leaking.
4. ...fabrics for blankets and clothing that prevent heat from escaping.

Page 40
1. nonrenewable; **2.** renewable; **3.** renewable
Word Alert! **1.** new; **2.** re-; **3.** -able; **4.** nonrenewable, "not able to be made new again"

Page 41
Students' reasons will vary.
1. Yes, it is a device with moving parts, powered by electricity.
2. Yes, it works with signals on tiny circuits.
3. Yes, it receives pictures and sounds sent as signals.
4. No, a computer is an electronic device. It has moving parts, like the keyboard and mouse, but it works with electric signals.
5. No, the first airplanes used motors, but no electronic controls.
6. Yes, many machines have electronic keypads.

Answer Key

Page 42

1. gravity; **2.** friction; **3.** friction; **4.** gravity; **5.** gravity
Challenge! Sample response: I leap off the dock and the force of gravity pulls me into the lake. I stand up and try to walk, but it is hard because of the force of friction of the water against my body.

Page 43

Students' drawings should show effort applied to one end of a prying bar to lift the load of a heavy rock. The bar can be balanced on a small rock or other object that works as a fulcrum. Captions label the load, effort, and fulcrum

Page 44

Sample responses:
1. ...pull down the menu under File.
2. ...its processor is like a brain putting together lots of information.
3. ...click on the icon for the program, which is a little picture.
4. ...new video games use a lot of memory, and the old computer doesn't have enough.

Look It Up! Sample responses: **1.** Both give you lists of choices. **2.** Both store pictures, words, and other information that you can pull up again.

Page 45

1. e; **2.** n; **3.** g; **4.** i; **5.** n; **6.** e; **7.** e; **8.** r
Answers spell *engineer*.

Page 46

1. shape; **2.** change; **3.** gone; **4.** list; **5.** pivot; **6.** purpose; **7.** image; **8.** tough
Antonyms to find in puzzle: finished, unreliable, flimsy, sameness

Language Arts

Page 48

Students use this page to assess their own knowledge of the term *compare and contrast*. Encourage students to explain how their drawing helps them remember what the term means.

Page 49

Sample responses for web:
Why: to find out more about something you're interested in
How: ask questions, find experts, read books and articles
Where: library, Internet, museums
What: collecting answers to questions, writing about facts

Page 50

1. suffix; **2.** prefix; **3.** prefix; **4.** suffix; **5.** prefix
Word Alert! Sample response: A prefix is a word part added "before" a word.

Page 51

Sample responses: **1.** cloudy, moist, gray; **2.** loudly, angrily; **3.** enormous, leafy; **4.** The boys hungrily ate the giant pizza.

Page 52

In the second sentence, the pronoun *it* is singular, so *It remind* should be *It reminds*;
Subject-verb agreement is needed in the third and fourth sentences: *vegetables tastes* should be *vegetables taste*, and *lawn look* should be *lawn looks*;
The pronoun *we* is plural, so *We lives* should be *We live*.
The subject of the last sentence is *things*, so the verb *makes* should be *make*.

Page 53

Underlines may vary.
1. as fast as the wind; simile
2. clouds are cotton balls; metaphor
3. like thunder; simile
4. right on the button; idiom
5. playroom is a trash dump; metaphor
6. raining cats and dogs; idiom
Challenge! Sample sentence following item 4: You have a mind like a steel trap!

Page 54

Students' reasons will vary.
1. No, folktales can have characters who don't try to trick others.
2. Yes, someone has to tell the story.
3. Yes, folktales have been passed down over many years.
4. No, a trickster usually does selfish things.
5. No, a trickster is a character that the narrator describes.
6. Yes, the narrator could say, "I will tell you about what happened to me."

Page 55

Sample responses: **1.** On a hot day, ice cream tastes great! **2.** Sarah's pets are a dog and a bird. **3.** mice, women; **4.** The three teachers' classrooms are next to each other.

Page 56

1. A; **2.** A; **3.** B; **4.** B; **5.** B

Page 57

Students' reasons will vary.
1. Yes, you summarize by telling the most important events.
2. No, the plot is the action, and the setting is where and when the action takes place.
3. Yes, suspense makes you eager to find out what happens next.
4. Yes, in a mystery, someone tries to solve a puzzle or a crime.
5. Yes, you summarize a plot by telling what the problem is, what happens, and whether the problem is solved.
Look It Up! Sample response: Suspense makes you feel as if you're hanging, or suspended, in mid-air.

Page 58

1. adjective, thesaurus, adjective; **2.** apostrophe, punctuation, apostrophe; **3.** conjunction, adverb, adverb; **4.** word origin, prefix, word origin; **5.** pronoun, subject, pronoun; **6.** similes, idioms, Idioms
Second activity: Students' sentences will vary.

Page 59

1. s; **2.** e; **3.** n; **4.** t; **5.** e; **6.** n; **7.** c; **8.** e
Answers spell *sentence*.

Page 60

1. suffix; **2.** pronoun; **3.** conjunction; **4.** folktale; **5.** thesaurus; **6.** research; **7.** metaphor; **8.** outline; **9.** essay
Answer to riddle: *unclearly*

Answer Key

History

Page 62
Students use this page to assess their own knowledge of *independence*. Encourage students to explain how their drawing helps them remember word meaning.

Page 63
Sample antonym for *conflict*: friendship
Sample example for *conflict*: Civil War
Sample synonym for *hardship*: troubles
Sample antonym for *hardship*: ease
Sample examples for *hardship*: not having enough food; not being warm in winter

Page 64
Sample responses in chart:
Primary Source: shows history from people who lived it; comes from the past; helps historians learn what people thought and did; president's speech, eyewitness account; diary; interview; letter; photos
Secondary Source: shows history from people who have studied it; written after the event; history textbook, encyclopedia; nonfiction book; talk by an expert; documentary
Both: learn about the past; read what people wrote; compare to the present

Page 65
1. Patriots; 2. Loyalists; 3. Loyalists; 4. Patriots; 5. Patriots
Word Alert! 1. patriot; patriotism; patriotic; 2. loyal; loyalty; loyally

Page 66
1. national; 2. international; 3. national; 4. international; 5. international
Word Alert! intercontinental. Sample oral sentence: We are taking an intercontinental flight to Europe.

Page 67
Students' reasons will vary.
1. No, they don't settle down long enough in one place.
2. No, they get food by hunting and gathering, not by farming.
3. Yes, agriculture and farming both have to do with growing crops.
4. No, corn comes from a plant, not an animal.
5. Yes, they move around as they hunt for animals and gather plants.
Look It Up! Students' definitions should reference wild animals hunted for food.

Page 68
1. rituals; 2. generation; 3. ancestor; 4. folklore; 5. heritage
Challenge! Sample response: My heritage comes from ancestors who came from China two generations ago.

Page 69
1. segregation; 2. equality; 3. protest; 4. integration; 5. debate
Challenge! Sample response: With segregation, different groups are like strangers, but with integration, they get to know each other better.

Page 70
Students' reasons will vary.

1. No, they wanted to start a settlement. Founding is not like finding.
2. Yes, a frontier is the edge of a settled place.
3. No, an inhabitant can live anywhere.
4. Yes, a pioneer and an explorer are both first in a new place. No, an explorer comes to learn about a place, but a pioneer might stay.
5. Yes, pioneers come to live in a new place.
Look It Up! 1. first settled; 2. did find

Page 71
1. treaty, ally; 2. irrigation, agriculture; 3. frontier; migration; 4. tradition, generation; 5. territory, statehood; 6. Patriots, militia
Second activity: Sentences will vary.

Page 72
Sample responses:
1. Parents and teachers pass down to children old stories about Paul Bunyan and Johnny Appleseed, who were heroes of the American West. These old tales belong to all Americans.
2. Native Americans lived in every region of North America. Some lived by hunting game and gathering plants. Others were farmers. Some groups formed friendships and others fought.
3. On July 4, Americans throughout the United States celebrate the birth of their country and freedom from Britain. They have picnics and fireworks and remember people like George Washington, who helped found the country.

Page 73
1. statehood; 2. segregation; 3. ancestor; 4. militia; 5. heritage; 6. protest; 7. conflict; 8. treaty; 9. hardship; 10. equality. Answer to riddle: in a dictionary

Page 74
1. treaty, agreement; 2. farming, agriculture; 3. partner, ally; 4. debate, argument; 5. scout, pioneer; 6. tradition, heritage; 7. equality, fairness; 8. migration, journey. Answer to message: If a job is worth doing, it's worth doing well! —a saying from folklore

Page 75
1. freedom; 2. region; 3. create; 4. global; 5. battle; 6. custom; 7. discuss; 8. roaming.
Antonyms to find in puzzle: segregation, difference, approve, enemy, Loyalist, ease

Page 76
1. h; 2. i; 3. s; 4. t; 5. o; 6. r; 7. i; 8. c
Second activity: historic

Geography

Page 78
Students use this page to assess their own knowledge of *region*. Encourage students to explain how their drawing helps them remember word meaning.

Answer Key

Page 79

Sample responses in chart:

for *drought*: a long period without rain; brown grass, muddy lakes, dead plants; People and animals can't survive long in a region that has drought.

for *vegetation*: grasses, plants, trees; green fields and lawns, gardens, thick forests; People and animals need vegetation to live.

Page 80

1. Antarctic; 2. Arctic; 3. Antarctic; 4. Antarctic; 5. Arctic

Look It Up! Sample response: arctic cold, arctic climate, arctic fox

Page 81

Students' reasons will vary.

1. No, the Arctic is in the northern hemisphere.
2. Yes, *hemisphere* means half of a sphere.
3. Yes, the equator crosses land, so you can step across it, even though it's not a real line.
4. No, the equator runs east-west, not north-south.
5. Yes, part of Brazil lies north of the equator, and the rest of Brazil lies south.
6. Yes, the United States is in the northern hemisphere.

Page 82

1. compass rose; 2. compass rose; 3. Latitude; 4. Longitude; 5. latitude; 6. longitude

Page 83

1. ...glaciers spread down from farther north.
2. ...lakes, valleys, and other physical features.
3. ...the low land called a canyon is narrower and has steeper sides than a valley.
4. ...a plateau is flat on top.
5. ...pass through a narrow waterway called a strait.

Page 84

1. A; 2. A; 3. B; 4. B; 5. A

Word Alert! Sample sentence: One example of how animals have adapted and are adaptable to cold weather is the adaptation of fur.

Page 85

Sample responses: 1. protect; 2. have roots; 3. has delivered; 4. a river; 5. the water supply

Word Alert! 1. wetlands: lands that are wet most or all of the year; 2. floodplains: flat land, or plains, that flood when a river overflows.

Page 86

1. adapt, Antarctic; 2. population, drought; 3. equator, tropics; 4. glaciers, latitudes; 5. vegetation, biome; 6. conservation, floodplain

Second activity: Sentences will vary.

Page 87

Students' reasons will vary.

1. Cross out *swamp*; it doesn't have to do with cold climates.
2. Cross out *adapt*; it's not part of a map.
3. Cross out *hemisphere*; it's not a physical feature.
4. Cross out *vegetation*; it's not a place.
5. Cross out *drought*; it's not a wet place.
6. Cross out *conservation*; it doesn't have to do with a map.

Challenge! Sample responses: 1. iceberg; 2. scale; 3. valley; 4. desert; 5. bay; 6. legend

Page 88

Answers spell *continents*.

Page 89

1. m; 2. o; 3. u; 4. n; 5. t; 6. a; 7. i; 8. n

Answers spell *mountain*.

Page 90

1. drought; 2. delta; 3. vegetation; 4. equator; 5. swamp; 6. tundra; 7. floodplain; 8. hemisphere; 9. tropics

Answer to riddle: Both have palms.

Civics and Economics

Page 92

Students use this page to assess their own knowledge of *industry*. Encourage students to explain how their drawing helps them remember word meaning.

Page 93

Sample responses for web:

What: Making payments to the government

Why: Government needs money to run programs, pay for army, fix roads, and more.

When: every year at income tax time, whenever you buy something, with every paycheck

How people feel: They want government to help them, so they know they have to pay it, but they don't like it.

Page 94

Sample responses:

1. ... is lower than demand, so people might pay a higher price if they can find the gadgets for sale.
2. ...did not exist, since nobody would pay such a high price for a cup of lemonade.
3. ...of oranges is lower than the demand.
4. ...go down, because the price is too high for people to pay, and they can find a different cereal.

Page 95

1. B; 2. A; 3. A; 4. A; 5. B

Page 96

Sample responses: 1. set up; 2. change; 3. government control; 4. be fair; 5. express opinions

Look It Up! Sample response: The Constitution is the document that sets up the United States government, but any nation or state can have a constitution.

Page 97

1. executive; 2. legislative; 3. judicial; 4. branches of government; 5. executive; 6. legislative; 7. judicial

Page 98

Students' reasons will vary.

1. Yes, workers make the goods or provide the services.
2. No, a carpenter's hammer is not made by nature.
3. Yes, a dentist needs tools and equipment.
4. Yes, human resources are the people who do the work.
5. No, but capital resources are made from natural resources like oil and metal.
6. No, a factory produces goods.

Answer Key

Page 99
Sample responses:
1. Supporters of women's right to vote worked for many years to change the U.S. law about voting. Women finally got the vote in 1920.
2. In our system of courts, some cases are tried before a judge. Other cases are heard by a group of citizens chosen for the trial. A person accused of a crime is entitled to be defended by a lawyer.
3. We read a news report that says state lawmakers want to raise taxes to protect water, trees, and other things that nature made. The state's governor and other leaders want to encourage business by lowering the taxes that businesses pay.

Challenge! The saying refers to colonists' objections to paying new taxes imposed by Britain. Colonists argued that they had no say in how Britain was governing them.

Page 100
1. industry, production; 2. demand, labor; 3. census, Constitution; 4. demand, supply; 5. executive, legislative; 6. capital resources, supply

Word Alert! legal/lawful; illegal/unlawful; legislation/laws; legislator/lawmaker; legislative/lawmaking

Page 101
1. s; 2. u; 3. f; 4. f; 5. r; 6. a; 7. g; 8. e
Answers spell *suffrage*.

Page 102
1. first ten amendments; 2. natural resources; 3. judicial matters; 4. legislative branch; 5. supply and demand; 6. suffrage amendment; 7. every ten years; 8. national law
Riddle and answer: What is always right in front of you, yet you can never see it? (your future)

The Arts

Page 104
Students use this page to assess their own knowledge of *expression*. Encourage students to explain how their drawing helps them remember word meaning.

Page 105
Sample synonyms for *rhythmical*: patterned, beating
Sample example for *rhythmical*: clapping along to a song
Sample synonyms for *improvise*: invent, create
Sample examples for *improvise*: make up words to a song; use leftovers to create a new dish

Page 106
Sample responses in chart:
for *loom*: a frame that holds yarn for weaving; long strings hanging from a bar with colors of yarn going in and out across the strings; to weave colorful designs or pictures on a cloth
for *textile*: a knitted or woven cloth; a large fabric hanging on a wall; to make fabric designs for clothing, furniture coverings, or artworks for decoration
Look It Up! Sample response: loom¹: a frame for weaving. loom²: to appear as a large shape that can't be seen clearly.

Page 107
Sample responses:
1. ...with her hand held high in the air, as if sweeping her servants away from her.
2. ...bent over, showing how humble and small he felt.
3. ...heavy and limp, to show the weight of his sadness.
4. ...stood straight and stiffly, and he shook his fist by his face.
Look It Up! The first part of *gesture* is like *jest*. The dictionary pronunciation shows *j*, not *g*.

Page 108
1. watercolor; 2. pastel; 3. watercolor; 4. pastel; 5. pastels; 6. watercolor

Page 109
1. A; 2. B; 3. A; 4. A; 5. B

Page 110
Sample responses:
1. ...the profile of a president facing left.
2. ...shapes in the background that seem farther away than in the front.
3. ...a portrait usually shows a person indoors.
4. ...use shading to make things seem as if they're in shadows.
Challenge! Pictures will vary.

Page 111
1. A; 2. B; 3. A; 4. B; 5. A; 6. A

Page 112
Students' reasons will vary.
1. Yes, when one actor says a line, that's a cue for another actor to enter or speak.
2. Yes, if scenes change, then the sets change.
3. No, the scenery is part of the set.
4. No, a flashlight is a prop, though flashing a light might be a cue.
5. No, they memorize their lines.
6. Yes, because an actor might hold it or do something with it.
Word Alert! Sample response: A theatrical property is an object that belongs to the theater.

Page 113
1. brass; 2. strings; 3. woodwinds; 4. percussion; 5. percussion; 6. brass
Second activity: Sentences will vary.

Page 114
Students' reasons will vary.
1. Cross out *loom*; it's not a kind of musical instrument.
2. Cross out *percussion*; it has to do with music, not with art.
3. Cross out *woodwind*; it's not a kind of artwork.
4. Cross out *stencil*; it doesn't have to do with a performance.
5. Cross out *pastel*; it has to do with a picture, not music.
6. Cross out *mural*; it doesn't tell about a musical or dance performance.

Page 115
1. c; 2. r; 3. e; 4. a; 5. t; 6. i; 7. v; 8. e
Answers spell *creative*.

Page 116
1. improvise; 2. woodwind; 3. stencil; 4. conductor; 5. brass; 6. rhythmical; 7. shading; 8. background; 9. watercolor; 10. script
Answer to question: visual arts

Science and Health **erosion**	Science and Health **lava**	Science and Health **magma**
Science and Health **organ**	Science and Health **tissue**	Science and Health **vibrate**
Science and Health **volume**	Science and Health **wavelength**	Technology **electronic**
Technology **friction**	Technology **gravity**	Technology **lever**

noun Rock heated to extremely high temperatures below the Earth's crust. Magma is molten, or melted by heat.

noun A form of molten rock that flows from a volcano.

noun The process by which rock and soil are moved from one location to another.

verb To move back and forth very quickly.

noun Groupings of similar cells that share a function in the body.

noun A part of a living thing that performs a function.

adjective Having to do with electric signals made by controlling the flow and direction of electric charges.

noun The distance between a point on one wave and a point in the same position on the next wave.

noun The loudness of a sound.

noun A simple machine made of a bar that turns on a support and is used to lift loads.

noun The force of attraction between objects, such as the Earth and the Sun, and between the Earth and objects on the Earth's surface.

noun A force that works against or slows down an object's motion.

Technology **mechanical**	Technology **nonrenewable**	Technology **renewable**
Language Arts **adjective**	Language Arts **adverb**	Language Arts **apostrophe**
Language Arts **idiom**	Language Arts **metaphor**	Language Arts **narrator**
Language Arts **plot**	Language Arts **pronoun**	Language Arts **simile**

adjective Having to do with an energy source or a natural resource that does not run out or that can grow again.

adjective Having to do with an energy source or a natural resource that cannot be replaced after it is used.

adjective Having to do with machines.

noun A mark that replaces missing letters in a contraction (*don't*), shows ownership (*David's*), or shows the plural of numbers and letters (*three X's*).

noun A word that describes a verb, an adjective, or another adverb.

noun A word that describes a noun or a pronoun.

noun A storyteller. A narrator can be a character in a story who uses pronouns such as *I* and *me* to tell what happens. A narrator can also be an unknown character outside the story who uses *he*, *she*, and *they* to tell what happens.

noun A kind of comparison in which one thing is said to be another.

noun A group of words or a saying that has a special meaning.

noun A kind of comparison, using *like* or *as*, that points out a similarity in things that are not usually thought of as alike.

noun A word that takes the place of a noun.

noun The action in a story. A plot often begins with a problem, continues with attempts to solve the problem, reaches a high point where the problem is or is not solved, and then drops to a conclusion.

History **ancestor**	History **conflict**	History **equality**
History **generation**	History **heritage**	History **independence**
History **inhabitant**	History **irrigation**	History **nomadic**
History **primary source**	History **secondary source**	History **tradition**

noun The state of being equal and having the same rights as others.

noun **1.** A dispute or lasting fight. **2.** A struggle between opposite feelings or beliefs. *verb* To differ or disagree.

noun A grandparent's parent or earlier person from whom one is descended.

noun Having self-government; not being ruled by another nation.

noun Ideas and things passed down over time.

noun **1.** All of the family members at the same level of descent from an ancestor. **2.** A period of about 30 years, the time between the birth of parents and the birth of their children.

adjective Moving from place to place in search of food; roaming.

noun The watering of crops using constructions, such as ditches and pipes.

noun Someone who lives in a particular place.

noun A belief or custom that is passed down from each generation to the next.

noun A report, article, painting, or other material that gives information about a historical event based on research of that event.

noun A diary, account, speech, photograph, letter, document, or other material that gives information about a historical event from the viewpoint of people who were involved in it.

Geography	Geography	Geography
adapt	**conservation**	**equator**
Geography	Geography	Geography
glacier	**hemisphere**	**population**
Geography	Civics and Economics	Civics and Economics
region	**amendment**	**branches of government**
Civics and Economics	Civics and Economics	Civics and Economics
Constitution	**natural resources**	**production**

noun The imaginary circle that runs east-west to divide the globe into a northern half and a southern half.

noun The protection and management of natural resources, natural environments, and wildlife.

verb To change one's body, behavior, or way of life in order to live in a changed environment.

noun All of the people living in a region.

noun Half of the globe. The globe has an eastern and a western hemisphere. It also has a northern and a southern hemisphere.

noun A great mass of ice formed from snow that has fallen over many years. A glacier moves slowly over land.

noun The three main groups that share power in the United States, as well as in other countries and states. The three groups are the lawmakers (legislative branch), the leaders who carry out the laws (executive branch), and the judges who make decisions about laws (judicial branch).

noun A change or an addition to a law, a bill, or a constitution.

noun 1. An area of the Earth's surface with shared characteristics. 2. Any area in which people share cultural elements, such as language, religion, or practices.

noun 1. The making of goods and services. 2. The goods or services produced by a business.

noun Sources provided by nature and used by people to make products.

noun The basic law of the United States. The Constitution lays out the system of government for the nation.

Civics and Economics **representation**	Civics and Economics **suffrage**	The Arts **collage**
The Arts **conductor**	The Arts **expression**	The Arts **orchestra**
The Arts **percussion**	The Arts **portrait**	The Arts **rhythmical**
The Arts **script**	The Arts **three-dimensional**	The Arts **two-dimensional**

noun A form of artwork in which bits of paper or other objects are pasted to a paper or other flat surface.

noun The right to vote.

noun The right to have lawmakers serve as the agents of citizens and express the citizens' views.

noun A large group of musicians who play together on various instruments and are led by a conductor.

noun The communication of ideas or feelings through artwork, music, dance, acting, and other forms of art.

noun The leader of an orchestra or a chorus. The conductor uses a baton to signal musicians or singers and to show the rate of speed at which the music should be played.

adjective Having a pattern that repeats in a regular way. Musical beats are rhythmical. Patterns of lines, shapes, and colors can be rhythmical. Movements and speech can be rhythmical, too.

noun A drawing, painting, or photograph of a real person, especially of the face.

noun, adjective The section of a band or an orchestra made of instruments that are struck, shaken, or scraped.

adjective Having length and width; flat.

adjective Having length, width, and depth. Also called 3-D.

noun The printed form of a play, movie, or broadcast. A script includes the words to be spoken, descriptions of the setting, and directions to the performers.